# WHEN 'CCO WAS COOKIN' BOOK

by DICK CHAPMAN

In the 1960s, '70s and '80s, WCCO Radio was "really cookin'." The recipe was one any broadcast property would covet. Many tried to discover the secret. Some came close. But none could quite capture the exact flavor.

# DEDICATION

It is sorely tempting to dedicate this book to my wife, Barbara, who certainly contributed to its creation. With my dexterity hampered by residual effects of Multiple Sclerosis, her nimble fingers conquered my computer keyboard when mine faltered. She urged me and inspired me to tackle this literary endeavor. She's my conscience. She's my life.

I could do worse than to dedicate this book to the Multiple Sclerosis Society which works so hard to help victims of this insidious and mysterious ailment live productive lives while working to find a cure. I've watched Society members toil while I served on the Minnesota Chapter's M.S. Board. If this book generates any profit, you can bet a portion will go to the Multiple Sclerosis Society.

But I must dedicate this book to WCCO Radio's legions of loyal listeners. There are none quite like them anywhere in the world. They are the people I've worked for, after all, for so many years.

# RECIPE INGREDIENTS

In alphabetical order, what made 'CCO cook, plus a dash of this person or that person, stirred in carefully at the precise time.

**ADAMS, CEDRIC**—A Legend in His Own Time. **BOONE, CHARLIE**—A Legend in His Own Mind. **BORMANN, JIM**—Smart Enough to Hire the Author. **BROWN, ROB**—Idea-Man Par Excellence. **CANNON, STEVE**—A Personality Split More Than Twice. **CHAPMAN, DICK**—A Humble Writer Headed for Greatness. **CHRISTENSEN, RAY**—The Boy Scout Motto, "Be Prepared!" **DEHAVEN, BOB**—The Gentle Giant—a Prince Among Paupers. **ERICKSON, ROGER**—A Mind in His Own Legend. **ERICKSON, JIM**—Radio's Rotund Recording Engineering Marvel. **FARMER, BILL**—Could Break Roger Up With a Mere Glance. **FLATLEY, PAUL**—The 'CCO Mildcat. **GIEL, PAUL**—What a Patsy! **GRANT, BUD**—The Old Trapper. **HAEG, LARRY**—The G.M. Who Knew the Territory. **HALL, HALSEY**—Holy Cow! They Broke the Mold. **HARTMAN, SID**—The Ink-Stained Wretch. **LAMONT, JOYCE**—'CCO'S Equal Opportunist. **PAGE, ALAN**—Not Your Everday Cardshark. **MERRIMAN, RANDY**—A Joke Book for a Mind. **NASH, JERGEN**—World's Most Professional Tightwad. **SPEECE, MAYNARD**—It's "teats" before 6 a.m. **STUCK, DICK**—"Under each snowmobile suit is a King Louie bowling shirt." **TARKENTON, FRAN**—The Georgia Peach. **TIBBITTS, BOB**—Coined the Yuletide Phrase, "Screw Thou, Tiny Tim!" **VAN BROCKLIN, NORM**—The Incredible Dutchman. **VIKEN, HOWARD**—The Guy Next Door. **VARIOUS** GOVERNORS, SENATORS, PRESIDENTS, DICTATORS AND DESPOTS.

# Table of Contents

# Table of Contents-continued

*When 'CCO Was Cookin' Book* includes 51 photographs, some from the files of WCCO Radio, which are reprinted by permission from WCCO Radio, and others from the personal files of Dick Chapman.

# PROLOGUE

Many younger readers never may have heard the voices of many of the WCCO Radio stars depicted in this book. Suffice it to say these people were giants in the world of broadcasting. Each contributed to the growth and development of a broadcast property that will be forever legendary.

There are countless other people not mentioned herein that did their share to perfect the WCCO Radio mystique. Those people ranged from secretaries to janitors—they are the WCCO family—I'm sorry to be unable to write about all of them.

Mystique is the proper word. Other broadcasters have tried and perhaps came close, but none ever captured the formula which caused each listener to think of WCCO Radio as "my station." Every on-air personality at WCCO Radio has received fan mail with the sentence, "I feel as if I know you!"

I hope these pages will help you get to know the great performers on the greatest radio station in the world.

**DICK CHAPMAN**

# ABOUT THE AUTHOR

Dick Chapman's mother insists she knew he was going to be a reporter very early in his life. She says he was an avid movie fan as a boy and when he reached the age when he could go to "the picture show" by himself, he would always return and tell anyone who'd listen all about the movie he'd just seen.

Mrs. Chapman says, "His eyes would just light up as he described the movie—complete with his own made-up sound effects."

Well, from 1950 at KFRU in Columbia, Missouri until 1993 at WCCO in Minneapolis-St. Paul, he found himself behind a microphone or before a TV camera—the last 36 of those years at WCCO Radio—a station Chapman called "The Only Game in Town."

His professional awards include the Lowell Thomas Good Youth News Award, the Sigma Delta Chi (Society of Professional Journalists) National Honor twice, the Columbia University Alfred I. Dupont Award, the prestigious Peabody Award and the Minnesota Page One Award.

It's true that those 36 years saw WCCO Radio become the most successful broadcast operation in the nation, basking in listeners that sometimes claimed 62 percent of all the radios turned on in the region. No operation has come even close to that.

Dick Chapman was there. He was part of it. And these pages tell the story.

**CEDRIC ADAMS**

# CEDRIC

Of all the personalities developed during the incredible growth of WCCO Radio, Cedric Adams was the most legendary. It's a fact—airline pilots crossing the skies of Minnesota, Wisconsin and the Dakotas watched homestead lights go out on the ground at precisely 10:15 pm when Cedric completed his "Nighttime News at 10."

He earned more than a quarter-million dollars per year in the days when a buck bought something—long before TV anchors negotiated contracts in the same ballpark with today's sports superstars. Hell!—in those days TV performers earned nowhere near what established radio performers were pulling down.

His Nighttime News was carried on stations in Fargo, Grand Forks, Minot, Mandan, Aberdeen and Sioux Falls in both Dakotas. The once-famous *Collier's Magazine* ran a full feature spread on him. Friends and business associates surprised him and his family with a Nicollet Hotel testimonial dinner and gave him a Cadillac.

Little did they know that Cedric's taste ran to the Rolls Royce Silver Cloud. He owned several of them a year at a time. He once told me a man was stupid to buy anything else if he could afford the first one, because he claimed he never sold one of his used Rolls Royces for less than he paid for it originally.

Thanks to the charisma and advertising abilities of the people like Cedric Adams, WCCO Radio was earning money that had back-East

Wallstreeters scratching their heads. They could not understand this small, privately held, corporation turning in such huge yearly profits.

We used to have a saying: "WCCO Radio makes the money. WCCO-TV spends it." There was even a nickname for WCCO Radio— "The Golden Goose."

Advertisers joined a waiting list to buy Cedric Adams as their spokesman—General Mills (Cedric sold all the Betty Crocker products), Wonder Bread, Peters Meats, Twin City Federal, Northwest Airlines—the list was neverending.

As a newcomer at WCCO Radio I was a writer for Cedric's newscasts. Frankly, I thought his voice was terrible. It was a little gravelly and a bit nasal. But, as I worked with the man I realized his secret charm. Cedric's interpretation from written copy to reception by the human ear was masterful. And, for him, it was natural.

Cedric was a "sight" reader—the best I ever encountered. He didn't have to "woodshed" his copy. That's a term for pre-reading. Cedric disdained that.

What Cedric Adams did was interpret his copy for himself—and in so doing delivered it perfectly to those on the other end of the radio. The purest form of communication is one person talking to another. That was Cedric's talent. He talked to his vast audience as though it were one person. And the vast audience—each one of them—felt Cedric was talking only to him or her. Many of us at 'CCO worked constantly to polish that "one-to-one" technique. For Cedric it just came naturally.

Cedric's "breakups" could fill an album—in fact they did! Since he was learning the contents of his newscasts as he read them, it was only natural that he'd break out laughing if something struck him funny. And if he really got to laughing (often, it turned out) I defy anyone listening not to break up themselves. His laugh sort of bubbled up from his belly until he couldn't control it. He wouldn't even try. It was infectious. You cannot describe Cedric's laugh on paper. You just had to hear it.

We used to write "kickers" to wind up Cedric's newscasts. "Kickers" are funny stories. That's the only part of his scripts Cedric wanted to see in advance. We soon learned never to let that happen because if he knew what was in the "kicker" he wouldn't interpret it right on the air. And worst of all he wouldn't break out laughing.

How often I watched him pick up a newscast and turn to the last page. "Not ready yet, Cedric," I'd lie, "It's coming."

We would actually hide the kickers and slip them in after Cedric was on the air.

Cedric was somewhat obese but not fat. He called himself "your rotund reporter." He wore horn-rimmed glasses and was full of life. He was a womanizer and at one time a hard drinker. He was not an alcoholic, despite reports that he had "taken the cure." He was only in his fifties when I first met him and I could tell he had learned to temper his drinking from his rowdier days. That's not to say he didn't throw a bender now and then—but never when it would affect his work.

He loved to eat, and loved to eat out. That meant from Mickey's Diner to Charlie's Cafe Exceptionale, to the Blue Horse, to the 620 Club—wherever. Restaurants named sandwiches after him. Charlie's had a Cedric Adams entree. The venerable 620 had a Cedric Adams Sandwich. Hey! The man had influence. With his newspaper column, he could make you or break you.

One of his pet projects became a crusade. Cedric Adams single-handedly brought about the ban on fireworks in the state of Minnesota. Some people say it was concern for the many childrens' injuries. Others think he just didn't like the noisy damn things.

Cedric's appeal did not go unnoticed nationwide. For a time he originated a daily CBS afternoon show, "Easy Five," from the 'CCO Studios. When CBS's legendary Arthur Godfrey wanted some vacation, he'd frequently call on Cedric Adams as a substitute.

Every celebrity who came to town beat a path to Cedric's door—which wasn't always easy to find. His schedule was so hectic he might broadcast his many newscasts from: 1. The normal radio studios. 2. An annex at the TV studios where he also performed. 3. His Edina home. 4. The offices of the Minneapolis Star & Tribune. 5. His famed boat on Lake Minnetonka. Cedric footed the bill to set those facilities up—even installing teletype circuits to each and hiring a full-timer to send the stuff out.

Cedric footed the bill for lots of extras. Never mind that WCCO Radio and WCCO-TV threw the traditional office Christmas parties each year—Cedric threw his own Christmas parties for the full staffs of each. They were always at Jax Cafe in "Nordeast" Minneapolis—one of Cedric's favorite watering holes. And they were not just Christmas parties, but formal costume deals. People came dressed as the Frankenstein monster, Cinderella, Zorro, Tarzan, Marie Antionette, Joan of Arc, Mickey and Minnie Mouse, the Northwest Bank Weatherball tower, and Santa Claus (usually Cedric himself).

I don't know the tab, but Cedric rented Jax's entire top floor and paid for the food spread, the cocktails, the wine and champagne, and topped it off with a top-notch local dance band. It was his thanks for all the behind-the-scene troops helping him throughout the year. On top of that, he gave personal gifts of champagne to his everyday writers at both radio and TV.

As one of his writers I appreciated it at the time, but now I wish he hadn't done it. There came a time later when writers were producing news copy for me. Every Christmas I got the same harrassment.

"Hey Chappy! Where's my champagne? Cedric always gave us champagne!"

Jergen Nash (as tight with a dollar as any man I've ever known, but more on that later) solved that problem by passing out bottles of Liebfraumilch. He tried to con his newswriters into thinking it was vintage German Reisling. I know you could get it then for about two bucks a jug.

Cedric's famous boat hosted celebrities often—celebrities like Godfrey, Bob Hope, Bing Crosby, Art Linkletter, Gene Autry, Eleanor Roosevelt, Zsa Zsa Gabor, and Esther Williams.

Oh, yes! Esther Williams was the beautiful, curvaceous mermaid of Hollywood who made her splash doing underwater musicals for the Silver Screen when that sort of thing meant box-office millions.

Something happened between Cedric and Esther. I never got the full story, but apparently a flirtatious dalliance went awry and Esther felt she had a score to settle with Cedric. Esther's appetite for leading men and husbands was well known in Hollywood—she was a lusty young woman. As time went by, she was a lusty older woman. And she could put away the booze with the best of them. (No wonder Cedric and she seemed to gravitate toward each other.) Whatever the roots of the incident, I was there at the wind-up—and it was something to witness.

The glamourous Esther Williams came to town hyping her own line of swimming pools. Cedric was still holding forth on his venerable 10 p.m. News and as luck would have it chose that particular night to deliver it from the WCCO Radio studios immediately adjoining the Minneapolis Athletic Club. As luck would have it that's where Esther Williams was hosting a cocktail bash.

Without warning Esther swept into the studios with an entourage befitting Queen Elizabeth. They all had been (ahem) drinking. Cedric was somewhat abashed but not overwhelmed. After all he'd dealt with the biggest of celebrities. He would think nothing of interrupting his newscasts to introduce a star, chat briefly, and pull one of his old tricks by inducing the celebrity to read one of his commercials—it was always great fun.

Cedric tried that on Esther. She didn't bite.

With one hand she pulled the microphone from Cedric and placed her other hand high on his inner thigh. She must have ad-libbed for two minutes as she stroked Cedric's leg. She purred such things as, "Oh Cedric, I hear you're so popular around here that housewives go to bed with you every night at 10. What is this appeal you have, Cedric? Can you share some with me?"

Cedric's usually infectuous laughter was reduced to a very nervous titter. He realized she was tipsy. He realized she was out to put him down. He realized he had made the mistake of offering her a live microphone and 50-thousand watts of power. I never saw Cedric sweat before that night.

Esther Williams got whatever revenge she was seeking but almost cost 'CCO its broadcast license in the process.

Once a year, the CBS Spot Sales Staff would visit. It was a big deal—several days of entertaining and touting our wares. The 'CCO talent was obliged to put together a sort of dog and pony show—introducing themselves to the network salesmen.

Cedric, one year, hired a stripper from the old Saddle Bar on Hennepin Avenue. She was pretty and petite except for her ample bosom which was what made her a star. Her nickname was "Penicillin."

'CCO's print advertising campaign in those days used the theme: " 'CCO—ACCEPTANCE!"

Cedric spirited Penicillin into the ladies room and then brought her into the studio, where presentations were underway, completely covered in a gunny sack. He delivered a spiel about the virtues of WCCO using a professor's pointing stick on some graphs he had prepared. At the finale, off came Penicillin's gunny sack revealing her adorned only with a glittering "C" over each breast, and a glittering "O" over her groin. Cedric pointed these out, whirled her around to reveal the glittering word "ACCEPTANCE" across her otherwise bare buttocks.

Sexist! You bet! But in those days few people (especially the CBS Spot Sales crew) even knew the concept of sexist.

Ironically, it was an effective sales pitch. And as the rowdy crew filed from the studio, Joyce Lamont was in the hallway. She never understood when Bob De Haven remarked, "We especially enjoyed your contribution, Joyce." Why did everyone laugh?

Cedric Adams died suddenly in 1961. His robust lifestyle may have contributed to the heart attack, but I think his work ethic may be suspect.

Consider this:

Cedric's day began early—a radio show before 7 a.m., his daily newspaper column, the Noontime News on radio, the 5 p.m. News on radio, the 6 p.m. News on TV, and the 10 p.m. Nightime News on radio. His only time off was Saturday (when he still wrote a column) and most of Sunday (when he still insisted on doing his beloved Nighttime News).

That daily schedule didn't include such extras as his travelling "Stairway to the Stars" amateur talent remote broadcasts or "Home Town Social", another weekly remote gig.

Cedric was yet again on remote in Southern Minnesota when the first jolt hit his heart. In confidence, I was told he charmed a nurse at a hospital to sneak him in a scotch and soda. The second heart attack later that evening claimed him. But Cedric, almost as if he knew, managed to enjoy his last cocktail.

## SOME FACES TO MATCH THE VOICES

In front: (left to right) **Franklin Hobbs** & **Maynard Speece**.

Second row: **Dick Chapman**, **Joyce Lamont**, **Joe McFarlin** & **Jergen Nash**.

Third row: **Ray Christensen**, **Steve Cannon**, **Howard Viken** & **Bill Diehl**.

At the rear: **Chuck Lilligren**. (Check out the nifty sportcoats!)

**HALSEY HALL**

# HALSEY

First of all his name was prounounced with the "s" in it—HalSey—not HallZey. Nobody got it right, except Halsey Hall himself and a few close friends. His father, grandfather and uncle were newspaper men. His mother was an actress who appeared with the great E. H. Sothern and Walter Hampden.

His very first "broadcast" experience was from a window on the second floor of his newspaper office where (with a megaphone) he yelled the round-by-round results of a heavyweight championship fight to an assemblage on the street below, reading from a wire service ticker tape. If I'm not mistaken it was the famous "long count" bout between Jack Dempsey and Gene Tunney from Boseman, Montana. Halsey was a boxing nut—a true expert. He hardly took notice of me as a new reporter until he learned that I had captured three boxing championships as a golden glover in my teens. After that, I was Halsey's boy.

One of the great Halsey stories (among many) was a boxing yarn from Manhattan. He was there with (among others) the veteran sports reporter Dick Cullum of the Minneapolis StarTribune. A heavyweight championship fight was scheduled, and Television was new! Wonder of wonders—you could watch the fight if you could just find a TV set. That was not an easy task in Manhattan—the bars or saloons that had installed TV were far and few between. Those that featured TV invariably were packed hours before round one.

Cullum said to Halsey, "Come with me and keep your mouth shut!"

They walked to a nearby bar with people spilling out the doorway. Cullum grabbed Halsey by the shoulders, turned him backwards and started backing into the bar uttering, "excuse me—coming out," with each backward step he took.

As Halsey related it, "So help me Hannah, the next thing I knew we were standing right in front of the TV set!" I confirmed the story later with Cullum who said, "Those New Yorkers aren't so smart."

Halsey did play-by-play from the ground up: High School football (where he termed the end-zone "the promised land"), Triple-A baseball with the old Minneapolis Millers and St. Paul Saints, Minnesota Gophers of course (probably where he developed his famous "Holy Cow" exclamation) and finally the Major Leagues with the Minnesota Twins. He nicknamed the famed slugger Harmon Killibrew, "the Brew", or just "Brew." Harmon loved it.

His fear of flying was legendary. Unlike John Madden, he conquered it—or at least struggled with it. Forced to fly by the oddities of major league scheduling, he purchased his first ticket with the phrase, "Gimme two chances to Baltimore."

On his initial flights he was known to take a pint of booze to a rear seat and cover his head with a blanket during takeoffs.

Colleagues recount a time he was caught without libation supplies in Chicago late on a Saturday and realized no liquor stores were open on Sunday.

With bottle shop closing hours nigh, Halsey nearly killed himself trying to run up a down escalator.

At the old Met Stadium, Halsey would enter the media's *Twins*

*Room*, stop first at the salad bar for a big handful of green onions and step immediately to the bar for a Manhattan where he would light up one of his famed cigars (he didn't smoke expensive ones). After his meal (perhaps accompanied with martinis), he would move on to the broadcast booth only after stuffing more green onions into his sportcoat pockets.

His play-by-play partner, Ray Scott, said, "On a hot day—with the onions, the cigars and whatever—it could get a little rank in there."

Once Halsey got his cigar and onions mixed up and set his sportcoat jacket pocket on fire. The Twins presented him with a custom-made asbestos sportjacket.

His laughter was infectious and he wasn't ashamed to laugh at himself—like the time he realized he was trying to broadcast into his stopwatch rather than his microphone.

His "pals" were often playing pranks on him. They caught him leaving a hotel shower naked and directed him through the wrong door to the outer hallway—locking the door behind him. A frantic Halsey pounded on the door while watching the elevator indicator climb and stop at his floor. Sure enough—four elderly ladies got out. Halsey got out of that jam by plastering himself against the wallpaper.

In New York, one day Dick Cullum tossed Halsey's hat out the hotel window. It landed near a trash can on the street below. Cullum swears a Manhattan bum wandered by, picked up the hat, looked it over, and tossed it into the trash can without even trying it on.

At a cocktail party one fine day, Halsey encountered a brash young reporter upbraiding a bartender for serving him a martini poured from a pre-mixed container. Halsey held court! First he reminded the lad that the cocktail was free (or as Halsey phrased it "gratis"). Then he expounded on the connoisseur's method for building martinis. "Martinis always should be pre-mixed," said Halsey, "The only debate is for how long." Halsey insisted you need not use the high-priced stuff (Beefeaters, Tanqueray-etc.) for a good martini. He favored ordinary Seagrams.

His recipe: Build your martini as dry as you wish, but never drier than 6 parts gin to 1 part vermouth. Put it in a closed container and refrigerate for at least 4 weeks. This allows the two ingredients to marry correctly. But always remember to return your martini to room temperature before adding ice (whether on the rocks or straight up) before consumption. You need some ice melt—otherwise the martini will knock your socks off. Halsey claimed some gourmet chefs insist on two months of a martini marriage before consumption.

Another story has it that Halsey was doing color at a Minneapolis Millers game and noticed an amorous young couple in the outfield bleachers. The game was somewhat boring so Halsey described their actvities by noting that "He kisses her on the strikes and she kisses him on the balls!" Old Hals denies he ever said that.

Ah, but Halsey had an incredible memory and was a master with the descriptive phrase. When the Brooklyn Dodgers were moved to Los Angeles, I watched him enter the WCCO newsroom, gasp at the wire story, then turn inward into his memories, scribble some notes on the wire copy and deliver an unbelievably brilliant 15-minute sportscast on that one story.

I'm proud that the very first air work I did on WCCO Radio was as a substitute for Halsey on that same "Time Out for Sports" broadcast heard every night for years at 10:15 p.m.

Halsey's talent as an emcee was sensational. Only Bob De Haven, Randy Merriman, and Roger Erickson were in his league—and none of them would deny Halsey was the champ. As an example, he was roasted once before a huge audience. After tons of gags it was Halsey's turn to reply. His opening remark was, "Well, a month ago when I first came up with this idea—."

The last time I saw him was at the old Twins Room. He was somewhat under the weather. A circulatory problem had required some vein surgery in his leg and he was walking with a cane.

"Halsey," I shouted, "Good to see ya—How ya doin'?"

He replied, "Just great, Chappy, me boy! All I need is a pinch-runner."

**BOB DE HAVEN**

# DE HAVEN

Big Bob De Haven was a prince of a man. He was known affectionately to his colleagues as "The Star," or just "Star." It was a nickname he gave himself and used frequently to spread his wry humor around the building.

Frequently, management would issue memos of varying importance but most often not much more than inane. De Haven would seek out the memo most prominently displayed on strategic bulletin boards and scrawl at the bottom:

### "APPROVED—★"

He wouldn't spell out STAR, just sketch a five-point star figure. There was a time managers didn't know who the culprit was, but the staff did. It did wonders to keep up morale. If De Haven didn't apply his "star" approval, everyone would read the memo carefully.

I loved and admired the man. I was brash enough later in my career to adopt my own nickname: "JUNIOR STAR." I did it as Bob did, scrawling "JR" before a five-point star figure. I'd even co-approve De Haven's approvals.

De Haven took me aside and said, "Chappy, you can be Junior Star, but promise me you'll never drop the "junior" until I'm dead." That's the type of guy he was. When De Haven did pass away, I never had the courage to drop the "junior." It would have seemed irreverent to such a great performer.

His first prominence was as "Friendly Fred," promoting Grain Belt Beer on his ever-so-listenable jazz music half-hour at 9:30 each night. But De Haven could do anything—news, interviews, sports, and, man, could he emcee. He had the knack of being able to read a live audience almost instantly. It didn't make any difference if the audience was 20 people or 20 thousand—he could warm up to them and make them warm to him within minutes of his opening gag. Believe me, that's a rare talent when performing before all sizes and all types of audiences.

I could tell on the air if De Haven was before an audience or in an empty studio. He just sounded happier if he was talking to live faces. He loved people. He loved audiences.

Some of his wit was contrived, such as his frequent references to his wife, "Hurricane Hat," and her many trips to rallies on her Harley Davidson. Some was spontaneous and quick as a whip, such as the time he finished a Northrup King seed corn commercial full of bushels per acre figures and asked Joyce Lamont what her yield was in her apartment balcony flower box. Mrs. De Haven, by the way, was anything but a "Hurricane Hat" type person. As proper a person as you'd ever expect to meet, she'd merely sigh and say, "To live with Bob De Haven, you have to take the De Haven with the De Haven."

Star was an excellent writer. It was he who conceived the idea of turning professional athlete when he retired as a broadcaster.

He backed it up with a fable about the struggling play-by-play announcer who put in years in Minot doing high school football, graduated to Three-I League baseball in Sioux Falls, finally making it to Triple-A baseball in Minneapolis. Lo and behold a job opened up in the Major Leagues—play-by-play for the St. Louis Cardinals. He flew down there, did a whale of a job in auditions, felt as though he finally arrived.

They hired Dizzy Dean.

I wish De Haven had turned pro athlete after radio. He was big enough to play tackle for the Vikings. But nobody had a heart as big.

**JOYCE LAMONT**

# JOYCE

It is said of Joyce Lamont that she once fled in panic before a scheduled speech lesson. It's true she was "mike shy" originally, but over her long career she became the most well-known female voice in 'CCO-land. Her obvious shyness contributed to her on-air effectiveness.

Unfortunately, she's a prime example of "equal pay" discrimination. Joyce performed monumental work while earning nowhere near the pay of her colleagues. Sadly, it's the way things were.

She broadcast recipes. She broadcast upcoming community events. She broadcast best buys at markets and shopping tips.

The community events were what kept WCCO Radio on small town Main Street. There were church bake sales, tractor pulls, quilting bees, bean feeds, fashion shows, amateur plays and contests. Anything going on from Bemidji to Balaton or from Rice Lake to Royalton, Joyce put on the air.

WCCO Radio's listenership backbone used to stretch right through southern Minnesota's farm belt, spilling into Wisconsin, the Dakotas and Iowa. Attention to those small communities had a lot to do with that.

When I say Joyce performed monumental work, consider this: Joyce received more than 10,000 cards and letters per month from more than 500 communities. She handled them virtually by herself. What a task to get everything of merit on the air.

You might think recipes on the radio is old hat and corny, but you don't know how many requests she received for copies. She also wrote her own cookbook.

If any proof is needed to attest to her popularity, consider that Joyce was featured on the Dayton's Musical Chimes broadcast and later (with Bob De Haven) on First Bank Notes. Both of those shows were in 'CCO's highest-priced prime-time period at 7:30 each morning.

I happen to know she's been chased around a desk by Cedric Adams, and dated Maynard Speece and others for a time, but she never married. Perhaps that's because she's always been happy being her own person.

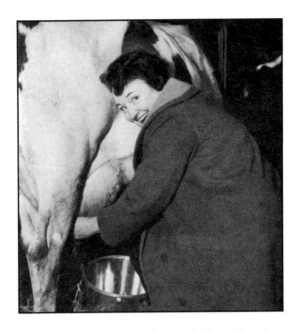

**Joyce** being a good sport at one of the WCCO Farm City Days.

**Joyce** and **Howard Viken** in the studio where Joyce co-hosted *First Bank Notes* with **Bob De Haven** and where **Joyce** had many feature segments during the **Howard Viken Show**.

**HOWARD VIKEN**

# VIKEN

Howard Viken is "the guy next door." He's the guy you borrow tools from. He's the guy you have a beer with. He's the guy you air your gripes to. He's the guy you swap jokes with. He's everyman.

His down to earth demeanor came through on the air. It just came naturally to him. He was the closest thing to the Cedric Adams phenomona—and indeed—the first Twin Cities announcer to climb into the lofty financial bracket akin to Cedric's.

He came out of Minneapolis North High School to the University of Minnesota and spent three years in the Marine Corps in the South Pacific during the big war.

That probably explains his early morning broadcasts when he'd yell, "Awright you guys, drop your clocks and grab your socks—let's go to breakfast!" Any ex-jarhead understood that little play on words.

He goes clear back to 1950 when as a rookie staff announcer he was called upon to introduce 'CCO stars at the picnic pavilion of the old Excelsior Amusement Park. Stars like "The Red River Valley Gang" (Musicians Dick Link, Ernie and Hal Garven, Burt Hansen, Wally Olson etc.), Clellan Card, Bob DeHaven, Stu MacPherson, and, of course, Cedric Adams. In awe of Cedric, Viken once said, "And now, here he is, Cedric Adams—brought to you by Meters Pete Products!" All announcers had problems with Peters Meat Products, because the dumb company insisted on the advertising motto: "YOU CAN'T BEAT PETERS MEAT!"

Viken paid his dues during the CBS owned-and-operated years. He was in the right place at the right time when CBS sold out and the new managment abandoned the stilted network "golden voice" style for more casual warmth that was to send WCCO Radio into orbit.

The "Howard Viken Show" drew 400,000 listeners on a given morning. WCCO Radio claimed an unheard of 62 percent of the market.

It's no wonder that Viken could virtually launch the career of a new comic named Bob Newhart. Newhart's hilarious record about "The Driving Instructor" enthralled Howard. He played it again and again. Listeners flocked to buy Newhart's humor. Ensuing Newhart hits included "The Grace L. Ferguson Airline and Storm Door Co." and the takeoff on Abner Doubleday trying to sell his idea of baseball to a game manufacturing company.

Viken and Newhart are friends to this day.

Viken did the same thing for Mitch Miller and his sing-along albums. Viken liked and played the albums. Listeners flocked to buy them.

Miller's record company received a single order for 50,000 albums from a Minneapolis-based distributor. Mitch later told Viken, "I thought they had at least one too many zeros."

Viken's timing also was right for what became known as "personalized commercials." These involved the broadcaster ad-libbing his pitch and virtually endorsing the product.

I did the very first one at WCCO Radio, selling Schweigert Meat Products during my 10 p.m. News. My grandparents were small-town butchers and I knew something about the art of making good sausage. I certainly knew what good sausage tasted like.

At any rate, I'd only been personalizing the Schweigert commercials a week or two when I got a phone call shortly after finishing the 10 p.m.

News. It was from Russ Lund, owner of Lunds supermarkets. He was calling from the island of Jamaica where he had just listened to my broadcast.

After bantering about how neat it was for the WCCO signal to reach clearly into Jamaica, Russ Lund asked if I could do the same personalized type commercials for Lunds. Well, of course I could!

Almost immediately, Lund bought into the 10 p.m. News. Soon thereafter, he bought Howard Viken. I think he bought Boone and Erickson too. I know for a fact that Lunds became the talk of the industry by establishing quality, up-scale markets—using primarily personalized radio as advertising. Prior to that, food stores used only print as their advertising method.

Viken's excellence as a personal spokesman brought him not only Lunds, but Northwestern National Banks, Piper Jaffray, Peterson Pontiac, Captain's Coffee and, of all things, Venus Waterbeds. Yes, he got one installed free.

Howard's wife, Mary, is a pretty good punster herself. She nicknamed that waterbed "The Dead Sea," never dreaming that Howard would repeat it on the air.

CBS Radio Star Arthur Godfrey elected to go to Vietnam with his close personal friend Retired General Curtis LeMay in 1966.

Viken was one of four CBS Station personalities asked to sit in for Godfrey for a week. He was all butterflies—not because of the nationwide audience—but because he would be performing alongside the statuesque blonde and beautiful singer Jane Morgan whom Viken had admired lasciviously for years.

Howard spiced up the frequent appearances of Joyce Lamont on his show by preceding her with a rowdy rendition of a tune called "The

Stripper." Obviously music for bumps and grinds, complete with shouts, applause and lewd whistles, Howard would say, "And now—direct from Duluth—let's hear it for JOYCE LAMONT!" It was perfect for Joyce's shy and demure personality.

One of Viken's more notorious off-color jokes involved his claiming a listener had given it to him, but he didn't get it. "Maybe you listeners get it, if you do, give me a call." The joke: "What's the definition of a mourner? A mourner is a nooner, only sooner." The switchboard lit up.

His most famous blooper came as he read a newscast about volcanic Mount Pentatubo. He said in an authorative voice, "Half the island was destroyed by a gigantic erection."

The switchboard erupted.

**Dick Chapman** (left) and **Howard Viken**. The newscasters and the talent have to work closely together. Split second timing is essential in radio. In this picture, I am signalling the engineer, "Now!" It may be a commercial, a live or tape insert into a news story, or the all-important meeting of the network at the top of the hour. This is when we would signal the engineers to make the moves. Now, the talent have to handle it themselves with computers.

**JIM BORMANN** (left) with **WALTER CRONKITE**

# BORMANN

Jim Bormann was WCCO Radio's News Director during the fabulous years when the station claimed more than 60 percent of the available listeners.

News was the backbone of that success story.

Bormann was an old school no-nonsense journalist. He wanted the five W's: Who, What, When, Where and Why. He wanted them up front. He wanted copy written for the ear. He wanted what he called "right now radio." If the story was in the morning paper, it was too old for the 5 p.m. newscast. With Jim's background heavily steeped in newspaper and wire-service work, it was a chore for him to develop his radio expertise. And, there were times he faltered.

During a long and bitter meat-packers strike at the old Wilson plant in Albert Lea, Jim got an exclusive telephone interview with Wilson's CEO in Chicago. Bormann elected to air it live during the Noontime News. He forgot about radio's time restrictions and filled the entire 15-minute newscast with the interview. He just got carried away. Unfortunately, the gist of the interview was heavily slanted toward management's stand on the strike issues.

I heard it as I drove toward Albert Lea on an assignment to interview union leaders and picket-line workers. They heard it too. In a station wagon clearly emblazoned with the 'CCO call letters, I wasn't exactly welcomed along the strike line. They didn't throw anything, but they sure waved a lot of signs. I was forced to opt for in-office interviews with union officers.

Bormann acknowledged some bad judgement and bent over backwards to get both sides of the story on the air later that day.

Jim Bormann is the man who hired me. He later promoted me to assistant news director and assigned me as the first full-time radio reporter at the Minnesota Legislature. Those were heady days.

Bormann and I covered the Minnesota DFL delegation to the 1960 Democratic National Convention in Los Angeles. You couldn't ask for a wilder scenario.

That week Minnesota Governor Orville Freeman nominated John F. Kennedy. Minnesota Senator Gene McCarthy nominated Adlai Stevenson and quickly switched his support to Lyndon Johnson. Bormann and I scooped the nation when Senator Hubert Humphrey leaked a decision to us that he intended to release his own presidential delegates (80 or so) to vote as they wished.

The Minnesota delegation was pro-Adlai Stevenson, except for young DFL turks like Gov. Freeman, Don Wozniak, and Joe Robbie (later to own the Miami Dolphins.) These guys kept urging the delegates to jump aboard the Kennedy bandwagon, lest it be too late.

I'll never forget an elevator ride with some delegates when Congressman John Blatnik climbed on at the 7th floor and proclaimed, "Guess what Gene McCarthy just did—came out for Lyndon Johnson!" I'll also not forget Art Naftalin, former Minneapolis Mayor who was Governor Freeman's Adminstrative Department chief at the time. I've always felt Naftalin was one of the more honest and capable politicians around.

Anyway, the delegation, on the convention floor, was flooded with pro-Adlai telegrams and mailings. The pro-Kennedy turks were circulating amid delegates claiming this was an organized media-type blitz. Gov. Freeman (Naftalin's boss) was a foot away when Naftalin looked up from a pile of letters and wires and said, "Bull Shit! These are grass roots people! I've looked through them all—they're too far apart to be part of a blitz—and I know half of them." Gov. Freeman was stunned. But at the time it was Naftalin, a DFL delegate, talking—not Gov. Freeman's Department head.

Bormann and I were invited to a post-session party in Senator Humphrey's Suite and got there before the hosts. Here came the entourage—Senator Humphrey and his wife, Muriel, and a batch of Congressmen yammering away on the politics of the hour.

Suddenly Muriel stopped, held up her arms and said, "Hold it! No more politics! We came up here to relax!" Whereupon she kicked of her shoes, one at a time—both of them hitting the ceiling.

A pregnant moment of complete silence until Hubert said, "Okay boys—Mama has spoken—no more shop talk."

And so help me, there wasn't.

Very few people know what I know about JFK's decision to pick Lyndon Johnson as his running mate. Frequently, Bormann and I separated to cover as much convention territory as possible.

Through my connections with the statehouse and Democratic powers formed during my years in Missouri's Capitol City, I learned that Kennedy planned to pick Missouri Senator Stu Symington as his Vice President. The logic was he needed the south, and Missouri's Symington would fill the bill while not alienating the Party's liberals.

When I approached Sen. Symington it was "no comment," but he couldn't hide a knowing smile on his face. My jubilant informers told me that Missouri's Governor at the time, Jim Tom Blair, would step down so that his Lt. Governor could appoint him to fill Symington's Senate term.

(Sound familiar, Minnesotans?) My Missouri sources said the deal was all set. They were planning celebrations and demonstrations.

When Jack Kennedy received the nomination, an army of Party pros beat a path to his door backing Lyndon Johnson for the number two ticket spot. Their message was simple and direct: "THE SOUTH—LYNDON GIVES US THE SOUTH!"

It didn't sit well with JFK. It was abominable to JFK's campaign-managing brother, Bobby Kennedy.

It wasn't until Lyndon Johnson himself approached Kennedy with the reasoning, "I want to be Vice President like I want another hole in my head—but without me, you don't win!" It wasn't until then that Kennedy decided. I'm told the Kennedy-Johnson meeting was top secret. I can't prove it even happened. But I know it was a flustered and rattled Kennedy that made his decision public at a hastily called news conference. It was not the poised and collected Kennedy we'd come to know. He didn't even answer any questions.

I know this: without LBJ's deliverance of half a dozen important southern states, John F. Kennedy would have lost that very close election to Richard M. Nixon.

Then Bormann and I were at the GOP Convention in Chicago. It was a cut-and-dried affair. Barry Goldwater stirred up some news with a fiery speech. There wasn't much news from the Minnesota GOP Delegation until rumor had it that veteran Congressman Walter Judd was on Dick Nixon's list as a possible V.P.

Nixon was holding court, calling in all the possibles for private chit chats. For Judd, it had to be a long shot. But yes—the call came—Mr. Nixon wants to see you. Congressman Judd, as experienced as he was in Party politics, couldn't conceal his excitement as he literally rushed out of the Convention hall. It's amazing what top-level politicking can do to a man.

Minnesota's other claim to fame at that convention was Elizabeth Heffelfinger, wife of grain-milling magnate Peavy Heffelfinger and long time Secretary to the GOP National Convention heirarchy. It was she who called the Role of States each year. She and her husband had contributed lots of money and lots of moxie to oil the Party machinery over the years.

For whatever reason, the Minnesota delegation conserved money by using part of the Heffelfingers' hotel suite for their infrequent caucuses. Bormann and I dutifully attended these, scraping hard for local news at the big event.

Following one such session, Bormann used one phone as I used another in a kind of parlor between the Heffelfinger's living room and their bedroom. All the delegates had drifted away. We finished our phone business and initiated our departure. I was glancing over some notes I had made as I followed Jim blindly. Suddenly Bormann stopped as he opened a door. I bumped into him from behind. Closing the door, he whirled and placed his finger to his lips.

"Wrong door," he whispered, "Quick—let's get out of here."

Bormann had mistakenly blundered into the Hefflefingers' bedroom. Apparently they assumed everybody was gone. Apparently, though Bormann never told me in detail, they were doing things that a husband and wife have every right to do in the privacy of their own bedroom.

Just a little sidelight of our diligent convention coverage that never made the air.

Jim Bormann was a newsman's newsman. He was a crusader for freedom of information, yet a defender of the right to privacy. He threatened to quit when management once tried to influence news content in the interest of advertisers. He was one of the founders of the Minnesota Press Club. He was an avid, if not expert, poker player. He was just a good all-around guy.

**A BUSY 1960 ELECTION NIGHT WRAP-UP**
Busy at election headquarters were, clockwise around the table, **Ron Handberg, Arv Johnson, Jim Bormann, Gary Bennyhoff, Clayton Kaufman**, and, back to camera, a news assistant. Dick Chapman was anchoring the various remote coverages from the 'CCO studios.

**RAY CHRISTENSEN**

# CHRISTENSEN

If one word could describe Ray Christensen, it would be "prepared." Preparation is his middle name. It's what probably sets him apart as a play-by-play announcer.

For his part, preparation is not just memorizing numbers worn by the various athletes. It is knowing something extra about every one of them. It is knowing the team strengths and weaknesses and the coaches' tendencies. It is whatever will improve his finished product on the air.

Ray's also a real gentleman—Mr. Niceguy—straight as an arrow.

He started at WCCO Radio in July of 1963. He says, "I'll do Gopher football and basketball as long as they let me."

At the end of 1993, he ceased other staff duties which included regular sportscasts, news, even staff announcing where he displayed an expertise in classical music.

One of his finest hours occurred during the infamous brawl that erupted during the Gopher-Ohio State basketball game at Williams Arena. Anyone in attendance knew it was the darkest hour for Minnesota sportsmanship.

Both teams were strong contenders for the Big Ten title. The game was a hard-fought see-saw affair.

At one point, several players hit the floor after a rebound went out of bounds. Gopher Ron Behagen offered his hand to the fallen Ohio State center, then pulled him up and delivered a strong knee to the groin. It was a sucker punch to end all sucker punches. The brawl broke out. Gopher players streamed off the bench. Fists were flying everywhere.

Christensen called it like it was—laying full blame on the Gophers. He called it a disaster. He called it the dregs of Gopher basketball.

Behagen would later claim his flagrant foul was in retribution for the Ohio State player having spit on him during the previous play. Nothing justified the groin kick, and Christensen said so.

Incidentally, one of the few Gophers who refused to join the fight was Dave Winfield. The huge Winfield probably could have mopped the floor with Buckeyes, but I'm sure he knew right from wrong. Winfield is destined for baseball's Hall of Fame.

Ray Christensen did a lot more than just sports for 'CCO. He did news, music shows and volunteered to substitute for anyone. I'll not soon forget one of those substitutions.

WCCO Radio hired many celebrities for week-long guest shots—people like comedians Morey Amsterdam or Louis Nye, the Homer and Jethro duo, Gene Autry's perennial sidekick Pat Butram, and Dagmar. Ah yes, Dagmar!

She was one of television's early stars—blond and busty—relegated to be a comic foil for male-chauvinist emcees. The "dumb blond" image was a million miles from the truth. She was bright, witty, warm and humble—talents that startled us all during her week guesting on various shows.

One of Dagmar's appearances occurred on an early weekday afternoon while Ray Christensen substituted for the regular host.

I sensed that straight-arrow Ray was a bit uncomfortable working so close to the statuesque Dagmar. I sensed his shyness. I felt Dagmar sensed it too. I became sure of it several days later when Dagmar was scheduled for a repeat with Ray on the same show.

Dagmar and her husband were staying at the Northstar Inn directly across 2nd Avenue from the WCCO Radio Building. I happened to be gazing out the newsroom window when Dagmar emerged. She was dressed to kill. Tight, short black dress, with deep cleavage. Black silk mesh stockings. Spike high heels and jewelry all over the place. Dagmar trotted across the street in mid-block, damn near causing a 16-car pile-up. It was the splashiest, most sensuous outfit she wore during her entire time at 'CCO Radio.

I have no doubt it was meant just for shy Ray Christensen.

Ray made it through the hour with Dagmar. His face was definitely rosier than normal. She crossed those shapely legs beneath that short skirt. Occassionally she bent low toward Ray's microphone, taking advantage of her decolletage. She was trying to loosen Ray up. I've never seen Ray as tense.

Ray's humor was dry. He was quick with it. You never knew when this shy, perfect gentleman was going to knock your socks off with a quick one. One of his best occurred in the newsroom when a veteran reporter, Bob Tibbitts, struggled with a telephone call. It was from a frantic (and I'm sure confused) woman who said she had seen a tornado funnel, but the twister was upside down. In frustration, Tibbitts relayed this to his newsroom buddies, and Ray said, "Tell her to go to the northeast corner of her attic."

Tibbitts just dropped the phone and laid his head on the desk.

**STEVE CANNON**

# CANNON

Steve Cannon spent half his career at KSTP as an arch rival to WCCO. When he made the switch, I'm sure Cannon thought he had died and gone to heaven.

At KSTP, Cannon plied his trade with expertise, and built himself a following; but when he switched to WCCO, he suddenly found his audience quadrupled.

Here was a totally different type performer by WCCO standards. Here was a man with a stable of voices which he used for brashness, shock effect, and something close to off-color radio. If Morgan Mundane, Ma Linger or Backlash LaRue went too far, it was their fault—not Cannon's.

Steve Cannon is so good at conversing with himself—via Morgan, Ma or Backlash—that more than a few listeners think the trio is real and in the studio with Steve. You know what? I think Steve sometimes thinks that himself—he's a multi-personality.

That's why Morgan, Ma and Backlash never accompany Steve to live performances at the State Fair. Steve doesn't like anyone to watch him work. It destroys the illusion and distracts from the intense concentration he needs to bring "all the little Cannons" off.

I remember once when a total stranger was standing in the hallway, peering into Cannon's studio. Cannon (during a break) stepped out and said sternly, "I'm sorry, I don't allow anyone to watch my show." The guy said,

"I'm not watching your show. I'm the contractor who's remodeling this joint. I'm looking at how to tear the walls out of your studio."

In truth, the concept of Morgan Mundane, Ma Linger, and Backlash LaRue came from the quirky brain of Eric Renwahl, an old Cannon drinking buddy and one-time newswriter at KSTP. I had a few pops with Renwahl myself over the years. He was an angling buddy and a true character. "Hurley's Hanging Gardens"—Cannon's Nordeast Minneapolis key club—was Renwahl's concept based on the one-time sin town of Hurley, Wisconsin. Cannon came up with the idea, "You don't need a key to get in—you need one to get out." Morgan's Alma Mater (The Electoral College) and his post as sports editor of The Congressional Record has Renwahl written all over them. Renwahl told me he invented Backlash LaRue based on an early cowboy star in the movies—Lash LaRue. Renwahl's fishing background just changed it to "Backlash."

I'm not putting Cannon down for this. These two guys collaborated to develop the Morgan-Ma-Backlash routine. And only Cannon could take those voices and characters to the heights they've reached.

There was a time—only once—when I witnessed Steve mix up his voices. Morgan asked Ma a question and Backlash answered. It flustered Steve so much he was forced to recover with a brilliant bit of coughing.

When Cannon first came aboard at WCCO Radio, I could only take about a half hour of him. I did the 4:30 p.m. news during his show. I'd be busy writing until air time and usually unprepared to chit-chat with Steve. He'd want to do something light and my first story might be a grizzly murder.

Steve's style was so aggressive I quickly learned that the best defense was an offense. I'd change the subject and throw him off track. I once complained of suffering from a "bacon string" injury. I told him I wasn't a good enough athlete to suffer a "ham string" injury. Ultimately, we learned to work together. And I must say, today Steve Cannon has mellowed and tailored and polished his material to be one of the premier stars of WCCO Radio.

**CHARLIE BOONE** (left) **& ROGER ERICKSON**

# BOONE & ERICKSON

Boone and Erickson—Charlie and Roger—these two were "the franchise" for quite a few years.

Recent developments found them not together as a team very often, which dampened their tremendous impact. But when they're together and when they're on, you can't beat 'em.

Charlie's road to 'CCO stardom is about as unlikely as you can imagine. He's the son of a New England preacher. He is a former choir boy who majored in theater arts and performed in the Repertory Theater at San Francisco State. Yet he ended up in radio at Fargo, North Dakota, hosting sock hops for teens about the time Rock 'n Roll was exploding.

Charlie won't soon forget having to cancel one of those affairs when Buddy Holly's airplane crashed on a flight from Clear Lake, Iowa, to Fargo.

From his Rock 'n' Roll background to WCCO required quite an adjustment. It's to Charlie's credit that his musical knowledge went far beyond Rock 'n' Roll.

The fact that he arrived at 'CCO about the same time as Roger Erickson was extremely fortunate. The mainstays of Charlie's voices were "The Senator" (Claghorn type), the "little kid," and "the down easterner from Maine." Those fit well into the miasma of voices Roger Erickson could do.

Charlie's not going to like this, but it's Roger who provided the creativity to write all the skits that quickly made the team famous.

Roger would wind up his early morning stint when the morning news block began at 7:00. He'd read all the newspapers available, looking for an idea for a current comedy skit. He'd find something—the man's a born comic. He's also a born entertainer. He has as much fun joking with two people in the hallway as he does gagging it up for a half-million radio listeners.

Roger also has that knack of touching the listener's pulse. Home-grown tomatoes, unkillable zucchini, brown chicken eggs, haylofts and manure spreaders—he could paint vivid word pictures based on his farm days in tiny Winthrop, Minnesota. Yet, he could reach the urban types with Charlie's Cafe Ordinaire, Bernadotte International Airport, and "Minnesota Hospital" (the longest running skit for the duo).

There's a Boone and Erickson intersection in one of the Twin Cities northern suburbs, especially named for them—a tribute to their popularity.

Southwest State University at Marshall gave them honorary degrees.

St. Paul Police "arrested" them for all the hard times they gave "Supermayor" Charlie McCarty. Then the Mayor "knighted" them. That's because of their hilarious spoof, "Bonnie Prince Charlie and the Knights of the Round Table," a comment on the colorful Mayor's administration.

They often spoofed Governor Rudy Perpich as the "Iron Ranger." Perpich was no dummy. He went along and reaped invaluable free air time by calling in live whenever he felt like it. Perpich invited Boone and Erickson to a sleepover at the Governor's Mansion .

Another classic skit featured Ebeneezer Scrooge chastising the NFL for scheduling games on Christmas Day.

There was a campaign to "Clothe the Animals."

There was "Halsey Hall at the Symphony." (Charlie does a good Halsey voice.)

Listeners to this day wait in anguish to discover if Dr. Whitney on "Minnesota Hospital" will ever entice nurse Helen to a romantic tryst in Brainerd.

They launched an area-wide drive to "Save the Skeet" after learning that a bunch of guys with shotguns were blasting those defenseless clay targets into the endangered species category.

Charlie's "The Senator" could get away with murder as they commented on the political goings on. It was always Charlie's best character.

Roger's protrayal of "August" (a 'CCO janitor) was arguably his best. August always knew the inside dirt at 'CCO. It gave the dynamic duo an avenue to poke fun at 'CCO's crack management team.

Roger created Dean Athelstan Milkhouse from the University's Agriculture Campus in St. Paul. It was an obvious takeoff on Athelstan Spillhaus, one of the U's most colorful and controversial professors.

The pair teamed to produce a holiday classic, "Lutefisk Lament." The parody on the slimey, ghastly Scandanavian tradition was so popular a record company snapped up the pair for a special record. It sold well.

Paranthetically, I must add something here. I'm a good trencherman and I've eaten everything from borscht to monkey gland steak—but I can't eat lutefisk! Believe me, I've tried. It may be the only food on Earth I absolutely won't eat.

Roger's name is synonomous with school closings. But it wasn't always that way. Before his arrival, a veteran newsman, Charlie Sarjeant, shouldered the task single-handedly. I'll never forget watching him write news on one typewriter, then swing to another after fielding another call closing a school. Back and forth on old manual typewriters. It was frantic—so frantic that once Charlie Sarjeant slammed the phone down so hard it ripped the whole contraption off the wall.

The system had to be changed, so Roger became 'CCO-land's official school closer whenever winter kicked up its heels. Now, 'CCO has a sophisticated reporting system when schools must close. Roger's machine-gun-like delivery is the end result. Few, if any, are as fast and accurate.

To guard against fraudulent school closings, only authorized school personnel can call the station; and they must identify themselves with a special code word. There are no such safeguards when weather gets so tough as to close businesses. That's why, in the midst of a dandy blizzard, Roger's hasty delivery resulted in "Veronica's Venetian Blinds are closed."

Opposites attract, they say. Charlie's suave. Roger's down home.

Charlie would review an opening night play at the Guthrie Theater. Roger would expound on the virtues of his antique one-cylinder John Deere tractor. Charlie would expound on the qualities of wine from California to France. Roger founded the BBFEP club: "Bring back fried eggplant." Charlie followed the top tennis stars, keeping everyone informed on the world's top tournaments. Roger was a died-in-the wool Gopher, Twins and Vikings fan—always a "homer" with blatant lack of objectivity. I don't think there's been a year when Roger hasn't predicted a Rose Bowl for his Gophers, a World Series for his Twins or a Super Bowl for his Vikings.

One St. Patrick's Day, Roger's quick mind came up with a new method of delivering the required station break, the every half-hour call letters. In his excellent Irish brogue, Roger would say, "You're listening to WCC (PAUSE) O'Radio."

Roger became the champion of gardeners the world over for his espousal of home grown tomatoes. He took pride in his own, grown in the fertile soil around Mound, Minnesota. That ignited the "tomato wars" between Roger and the famed Augie Mader, who raised some beauties near St. Bonifacius. The fight was over who'd produce the first ripe tomatoes and who'd produce the biggest.

I live in Mound myself, and I jumped into the war with my secret weapon—buckets of water from Lake Minnetonka applied to my plants. Besides, I cheated by purchasing starting plants already containing blossoms. Roger discovered that "no no," which probably explains why he snubbed me when I proposed we build a "zucchinol" plant in Mound. Mound is the zucchini Capital of the World. Why not make "zucchinol" as a gasoline additive like the corn growers do?

For decades, listeners enjoyed (I think) the "Good Morning Song" shortly after 6 a.m. Maynard Speece and Jergen Nash had been belting it out for years, but Roger refined it to a classic. Church choirs sent us their own taped versions. The St. Paul Chamber Orchestra did an outstanding version. It was grand. It became an honor to join in the daily sing-a-long.

One morning Roger was absent and his co-hort Dave Lee insisted I abandon the news room and sing with him. I'm not exactly a Pavarotti. After the lead-in, Lee clammed up. I was forced to sing the hallowed "Good Morning Song" a cappella. What agony! Such indignity! Your turn is coming, Dave Lee. I'll get you one day!

For 35 years it's been, as Charlie often says at show's close, "Boone and Erickson, a legend in their own minds."

**JERGEN NASH**

# JERGEN

"Good Evening, Ladies and Gentlemen—this is Jergen Nash." That rich voice spoke those words every weeknight at 9:30 for a good many years. It was the opening to "Jergen Nash Presents," a half-hour light classic music show that the Rock 'n' Roll set couldn't stomach. Others could. It sure lasted a long time.

He was so corny that he used to invite housewives listening to waltz around the kitchen with him at noontime. With the waltz playing he'd say, "Watch the corner of the table. Oops, almost tripped over the mop." Corny enough that his noontime gig lasted almost ten years.

But Jergen's true love was news. His voice was perfect for it. He was the ultimate professional—authoritative, believable—I can count his script flubs on one hand.

But when he did flub, it could be monumental. There was the time at our State Fair broadcast booth when technicians removed one of two microphones. Jergen didn't notice. He flipped the mike switch where there was no mike, and spoke for nearly two minutes into mid-air. That translated to dead air for WCCO Radio. Jergen didn't know because he had also neglected his head set.

And there was a newscast sponsored by his long time sponsor, Twin City Federal. TCF and Midwest Federal were in serious competition—spending heavy advertising dollars. Both had commissioned catchy musical jingles to intro their commercials. Jergen signaled for the Twin City Federal jingle, but the technician played the Midwest Federal jingle. Totally mortified, Jergen punched open the mike (I think he wanted the intercom) and shouted across our 50-thousand watts, "STOP THE MUSIC!"

He had an abiding love for food and drink. He had that rare metabolism that allowed him to eat anything, in any amount, and never add a pound to his lanky frame. He loved wine and beer, but never overindulged on either. Maybe that was because he had such an enormous tank that treated alcohol the same as food. He never got tipsy. We used to cooperate to brew our own beer. It was fun. But more importantly for Jergen, it was cheap.

Yes, it's true. I've never met anyone so tight with a penny. It was a point of honor to him.

Jergen actually saved his VFW Buddy Poppy from year to year so he could walk right by the hawkers on the street. His poppy was so old it was still made of paper and had lost much of its color. Nonetheless, he'd haul it out on Poppy Day, and carefully stow it away for next year. Never mind that Jergen was an overseas veteran himself. He met his marvelous Welsh wife, Mary, in London during World War II.

Jergen made a six-block walk each noontime to avail himself of a low-cost lunch special at a downtown eatery. One day the lunch counter was struck by an outbreak of hepatitus. Egad! Jergen hastened to his doctor for an anti-hepatitus shot.

A day later, Hennepin County offered free immunization shots to patrons of the lunch spot. Jergen was outraged. He called the County to see if they'd reimburse him for his personal doctor's fee. It was a point of honor.

Jergen and his wife shared a philosophy of liberalism. Both contributed time and money (yes, Jergen's money) to worthy liberal causes. But Jergen remained absolutely objective and neutral where his work was concerned.

After retiring from regular duties, he continued for years writing and delivering his own nostalgic little program on Sunday mornings. They were sometimes serious, sometimes whimsical, always quite listenable.

Virtually no one knew that the man had been stricken by cancer until his final broadcast, when he said "an illness" had sapped his strength and stamina to the point he felt unable to continue. It was a gut-wrenching performance. Jergen, the ultimate professional, delivered his farewell without a tear, with his undeniable dignity. He died within the week.

**SID HARTMAN**

# SID

What can I say about Sid Hartman?

Well, flat out, I can say he's one of the hardest working guys I've ever seen in this business.

Just read one of his columns and figure how much work is involved to amass all the little odds and ends he sticks in at the end. Does he ever take a vacation? What does it take to pile up all those "close personal friends"? Combine his broadcast work with his newspaper work and there's not much time for him to handle his financial empire.

I can also say he's got a heart—but he seldom shows it.

My first Hartman encounter was when I was a WCCO Radio rookie. Time available for staffers to do tape-recording and editing has always been at a premium. Hartman always has had the annoying habit of throwing his weight around to get studio time at a moment's notice.

I was in a studio, recording a news interview by telephone when Hartman barged into my broadcast booth demanding I get lost for something urgent he had going. Rookie or not, I was outraged for anyone to barge into a live sound studio.

I asked my interview to wait. I'm sure my face was bright red. I clenched my fist, drew it back, and came out of my chair with the full intention to put Hartman on the deck. He fled.

A few days later he apologized. Since that time Hartman and I have gotten along fine.

Sid seldom is intimidated by anyone. He's dealt with Gopher coaches from Bierman to Holtz to Kundla to Wacker. He's done Twins managers from Cookie Lavagetto to Tom Kelly. And he did all the Viking coaches, including the incomparable Norm Van Brocklin—Sid's one and only nemiesis—the one man who could (and often did) intimidate Sid Hartman.

After all, Van Brocklin was overwhelming. Swear words flowed from his lips like poetry. Vikings fans seated behind the team bench eschewed the poor sight lines so they could hear Van Brocklin's frequent tirades against a player who screwed up. He put a whole new meaning into the art of cussing. Viking Coach Jerry Burns was pretty blue himself—but nowhere near Van Brocklin's league.

I once attended a media function (cocktails and canapes) at the Viking main office in Bloomington. I happened upon an unbelievable scene involving Van Brocklin and WCCO-TV News Director Rollie Johnson. Rollie himself had a way with salty language. Van Brocklin and Rollie had become close friends as drinking and fishing buddies.

I'll never know what precipitated this, but as I parked my car I spied Norm Van Brocklin standing on the hood of Rollie Johnson's car. He was urinating on the windshield shouting, "Piss on you, Johnson!"

Rollie was locked inside, with the windshield wipers going, shouting "Up yours, Van Brocklin!" (Actually, the language was harsher, but the hand-signal was unmistakable.)

Perhaps you now sense Van Brocklin's explosive nature.

Picture, then, a Monday morning at WCCO Radio where Sid Hartman has the unenviable task to tape a Van Brocklin interview on a call to Los Angeles. It's six a.m. on the west coast. The Vikings had been buried by the Rams the previous day, thanks in part to a terrible performance from running back Tommy Mason who fumbled three times. I happened to be on hand as Hartman made the connection in Van Brocklin's hotel room. Here's how it went:

Van Brocklin: "Hullo!" (Sleep dripping from his voice.)

Hartman: "Sid Hartman, Coach, we gotta do your show."

Van Brocklin: "Jesus Christ! What time is it? I gotta wake up to some Black Irishman!"

Hartman: "Sorry, Coach, it's the only time I can call."

Van Brocklin: "Shit! (A few other choice expletives, punctuated by coughs, belches and throat clearing.) Okay! Let's get it over with."

Now the classic Hartman question: "How about that Tommy Mason?"

Van Brocklin: "Goddam it! What kinda question is that! How about him! How about 10 other guys! How about the Rams! We got our ass kicked!" (Van Brocklin ranted on for what seemed like 5 minutes turning the air blue with his vitriolic language.)

Finally Hartman (in a meek voice): "Whataya want me to ask you, Coach?"

Think what you will about Sid Hartman. He's left his mark.

**RANDY MERRIMAN**

# RANDY MERRIMAN

Randy Merriman was one of the great pitchmen of all times. I think in his heart he always wanted to be a stand-up comedian. As a lad, he was–going almost as far back as vaudeville. He worked local theaters, lodge meetings, amateur nights, finally catching on at KSTP in St. Paul.

He became a national star of one of the industry's quiz shows, "The Big Payoff," a network success co-starring former Miss America Bess Myerson, whose main contribution was modeling the mink coats given away as the show's grand prize.

He was flying high in the '50s until the quiz show scandals erupted in the '60s.

"The Big Payoff" escaped the scandals, but Randy told me he got out because he knew there was skullduggery going on. He thinks contestants that producers wanted were given reference books pertaining to upcoming questions. That's how they kept the more colorful contestants and booted the duds.

Randy was not involved, but he knew his reputation would be sullied if it ever came out.

It wasn't his only reason for seeking a return to Minnesota. His kids were high school age, and mid-town Manhattan didn't offer much choice for education. Besides, he'd made a tidy bundle, invested it well, and felt he could sort of semi-retire back home in Minnesota doing his thing. It worked well for both him and WCCO Radio.

We first worked together on a thing called, "The Randy Merriman Matinee." It was one of the last 'CCO broadcasts featuring live musicians. Wally Olson directed the likes of Burt Hanson, Dick Link, Willie Peterson and his incredible wife Jeanne Arland Peterson, one of the great jazz pianists of our time. The Peterson kids are headliners in the biz today.

All I did on the show were five-minute newscasts. But the gregarious Merriman wouldn't let me on and off the show without some verbal horseplay. We hit it off. It worked. WCCO Radio's image was changing from the stodgy, formal style of the CBS owned-and-operated days, to a warmer, more human form of communication. We were giving something of ourselves to the listener. I can't tell you how many fan letters I have containing the phrase, "I feel as if I know you." And I wasn't the only one.

By now the quiz show scandal was toppling such hits as "The $64,000 Question" like dominoes.

It was then that General Manager Larry Haeg conceived an idea for a quiz show called "Honest to Goodness." He capitalized on the nationwide scandal. WCCO Radio would show the world there's decency and fairness in the broadcast industry.

"Honest to Goodness" paid in multiples of a paltry $8.30 (the station's dial location) and furthermore posted the correct answers for anyone to see at participating sponsors' locations (not a shabby marketing idea).

He called upon Merriman and me to co-emcee the show at 9 p.m. each evening.

Why me? I'm the guy who had to dig up all the questions.

I must admit, Randy and I were lukewarm to the format. It was clumsy, and the listeners were virtually always ready with the correct answers. I was overwhelmed trying to keep us supplied with questions, and there was little suspense since the jackpot seldom grew beyond $8.30.

We ceased posting the answers. I dug up tougher questions.

All of a sudden we had a hit on our hands. We actually posted ratings higher than prime-time television.

"Honest to Goodness" rose and fell based on who was on the other end of the telephone. Never mind Merriman and me, the stars of the show were the contestants. Admittedly, we (especially Merriman) had to draw out the contestants' qualities—but people listened just to hear what quaint or weird neighbor was going to be quizzed next.

And there were some dandies.

We had a dowager seeking a husband. We had a widower seeking a dowager. We had working girls, we had truckdrivers, we had youngsters and oldsters.

One guy was a chicken plucker. He said he wanted to get his hands on Abner's chicken. Abner was Randy's nickname for our technical engineer who had the annoying, if amusing, habit of inserting this rooster sound effect into our broadcasts whenever the whim hit him.

We occasionally found listeners who were into the sauce—some admittedly, others obviously. One guy even hiccupped, as though on cue.

One young man's mother couldn't come to the phone because she was asleep in the bedroom with "Uncle Charlie."

I'd place each call and chat just long enough with the listener for Merriman to get a feel for the personality. He was excellent at it.

One of the classics was a man we caught atop a ladder painting his kitchen. His wife was out, leaving him to baby sit. Merriman painted a wonderful word picture.

"You're sitting on top the ladder right now?"

"Yeah—the phone's right here on the wall."

Merriman posed the question worth something like $41.50.

What happened next you couldn't have scripted.

The contestant said, "Hang on a second. My wife left the answer around here somewhere."

Then—a resounding crash! Kids started yelling! A mild curse word may have slipped out. Pandemonium!

Merriman is milking it, "Mr. Smith! Mr. Smith! Are you all right?"

Finally, the guy gropes the clacking phone back to his head and says, "Oh Geez! I kicked the paint over on the counter. My wife's gonna kill me!"

Merriman opined that maybe he could clean it up before she got back.

"No, not that," he said, "I dumped the paint all over the answer. That's why she's gonna kill me!"

Then there was the Irish wake.

A guy named Murphy had sent in the customary postcard asking to be called. When we called it was Mrs. Murphy who answered. Merriman chatted amicably with her. She seemed to be a delightful lady—cheery and relaxed.

Finally Randy asked, "Is your husband home?"

Her nonchalant reply, "Yes, he's in the living room."

"May we speak to him?"

"No."

"Why not?"

"He's dead!"

Can you believe it? We were chatting along in the midst of an Irish wake. Mr. Murphy was in his coffin in the living room.

Merriman was dumbfounded. He almost came apart. He apologized profusely, expressed his condolences, begged forgiveness. Mrs. Murphy remained silent until Randy tried to ring off.

"Wait a minute," she said, "Don't I get a chance to answer the question?"

What would you do? Merriman stumbled all over himself regaining composure long enough to pose the question.

Mrs. Murphy didn't have the correct answer—but she thanked us for calling.

Occasionally we broadcast what we called "Clear Channel Honest to Goodness." It was to accommodate the listeners whose postcards came from far away—often well outside 'CCO's primary broadcast area. "Clear Channel" referred to WCCO's federal designation as the only station allowed to broadcast on the 830 dial location. There were only twelve such stations in the nation, and when added to 50-thousand watts, it threw that signal far and wide. Postcards were not uncommon from Texas, Pennsylvania, New York, Vermont, Alabama, Virginia. One guy said he was sitting in his car outside the White House and we came in like a local in Washington D.C.

It was during one of those broadcasts we called a young man in Flin Flon, Manitoba in Canada. I'd been to Flin Flon on one of my more exotic fishing expeditions. Pretty place in the Summer—lots of towering pines and clear lakes.  But we were calling in February.

The young man's father answered the phone.

"Oh, Yeah—Honest to Goodness—Jimmy and I listen all the time. Ain't much else comes in good up here, aye."

Digging into my best interview technique, I asked, "How cold is it tonight in Flin Flon?"

He said, "Man, it's so cold it's comin' through the walls!"

Well, for the next few minutes Merriman and I and the father expounded on cold weather. The Canadian didn't have exact figures, but he knew it was at least 40-below with a wind of at least 40 miles-per-hour. Wind chill must have been off the chart. The guy had his furnace on full, and a roaring fire in the fireplace, but the cold was still coming through the walls.

Time was running short on our broadcast so we were anxious to talk to Jimmy so we could ask the question. Get this!

"Jimmy ain't here. He's outside—down the driveway, waitin' for the bus."

"What!"

"Yeah, he's goin' over to see his girlfriend. You know these teenagers, aye. I'll try the question for him."

He didn't have the right answer either.

That happened as the show closed Friday night. Between then and our next broadcast the following Monday, our switchboard was inundated with calls demanding to know what became of Jimmy. The Monday morning mail was packed with cards and letters asking the same thing. Many were somewhat threatening.

Nothing would do but we call Jimmy in Flin Flon that Monday night. Thankfully he was there. Thankfully he had enjoyed a nice visit with his girlfriend. Yeah, it was cold—but he had his snowmobile suit and good boots. Thankfully he still had all his fingers and toes. Why wait in the cold for a bus? Couldn't get the pick-up started.

Oh yes, Jimmy didn't have the right answer either. Merriman gave him $8.30 anyway, suggesting it might go for cab fare instead of the bus next time.

On another cold winter night one of my casual remarks triggered the most amazing listener reaction we'd ever encountered.

I remarked to Randy that I was a compulsive chunk-kicker. I explained that what I termed a "chunk" is that conglomeration of packed snow, slush and ice that forms behind the tires of vehicles during the winter. I confessed to having this uncontrollable urge to kick them until they dropped off.

Bingo! It turned out there are uncounted thousands (maybe millions) with the same psychotic quirk.

Listeners confessed on the air as to how chunk-kicking allowed them to release stress, blow off steam, uncork their frustrations. Fans wrote us about it. What northerner or transplanted Sun-belter, at one time or another, hasn't taken a good healthy kick at one of those things? During tough winters, when cabin fever sets in, it can become an addiction. We had created a whole new winter sport.

Randy and I founded the IAPCK—International Association of Professional Chunk Kickers. The sport of chunk-kicking was launched. Merriman and I made up the rules and declared ourselves World Champions.

We defined a legal chunk as a mass of material made up of compacted snow and ice, blended with dirt, gravel, salt, decayed leaves, fertilizer, oil, gum-wrappers, small coins, a few keys, an occasional dinner ring and various vitamins and minerals. To be eligible for professional competition the mass must weigh at least two stones.

Chunks can be as hard as manganese steel or soft as lemon-lime sherbet. They can be small or massive, sleek or irregularly shaped. They might be grotesquely ugly or smoothly sharp-pointed and glisteningly beautiful (these usually behind the front tires of 1966 Thunderbirds).

Scoring in chunk-kicking is based on just how quickly and efficiently you dislodge said chunks, tempered by your style and grace.

Chunks come and go depending on the whims of winter. You have to have regular snowfalls, but the chunk crop depends on alternate freezing and thawing, snow removal techniques, the wind-chill factor, type of tire treads, and how many hills there are for people to get stuck on. Randy and I used to issue chunk-kicker alerts as part of our weather forecasts.

Randy and I claimed to have chunked all over the world and beaten all comers. The sport actually became an official event of the St, Paul Winter Carnival. We out-kicked Governor Karl Rolvaag and Public Works Commissioner Milt Rosen in downtown St. Paul. The event was broadcast live by 'CCO's Ray Christensen with Sports Director Paul Giel doing color.

Wirt Wilson Insurance Company sponsored the broadcast and actually created a policy to guard against vehicle damage or medical bills occasionally incurred to kickers' toes, insteps or shins. Merriman wore a huge German Lodencoat bedecked with fake kicking medals and sported an oversize pair of white bunny boots with gold gilded toes. I had sparkly spangles on my boots. It was great fun.

We also fantasized (lied) about our exploits on the air. There was the Mesabi Iron Range Chunk Off, when Randy's deadly accuracy and my stunning style beat the famed "Iron Toe" Saarinen (The Finnish Fiend) and his partner "Mighty Moe" Modewleski, a Polish soccer-style side-winder. We nipped them in overtime when Merriman dropped a chunk of ten stone with a single skidding front cross-over, and I scored 28 style points with my best one-and-a-half turn around back-kicks.

Who could forget the International Falls Invitational when we beat Jaques Le Stroppe (a ringer from Ontario) and Ole Olafson (a jack pine savage from somewhere north of Warroad). Experience paid off then. Having won the coin toss, we avoided a black 1963 Impala which had been absorbing the heat of the sun. (Light paint jobs reflect the heat. Dark paint absorbs and transfers heat right into the chunks.) Olafson dislocated his toe launching a thunderous kick at a 12-stone monster beneath the rear fender. Ole's big foot went through that softened chunk like a sledge through butter, smack against the suspension spring. With Olafson sidelined, the Canadian ringer was no match for us.

Listeners asked if chunk kicking was legal in inside parking ramps. We decreed that true chunk kicking is done out of doors where the chunk-chill factor comes into play. Some splinter leagues had been kicking indoors. The IAPCK didn't recognize them.

As our fame grew we received tons of mail.

A farmer chided us that he'd kicked chunks long before there were cars. But those were unique frozen organic chunks found in farm fields. He claimed he could kick 'em all the way to school and back.

One writer dropped not only his chunk, but the entire exhaust and manifold system with a single kick. He enclosed a repair bill and a demand for restitution.

The most graphic letter came from a lady in Minneapolis (freshly relocated from Elmira, New York). It was about her Uncle Ferd (a pioneer chunker) who had returned victorious after beating the fearless Ivan Ivanhoff in Moscow. She said they had chunked for two days and two nights in a dead tie, until the judges discovered Ivan was barefoot and had filed his toenails to a razor sharpness. Even the Soviets have rubles—er—scruples, so Fearless Ivan Ivanhoff was disqualified and assigned to doing ice sculptures in Siberia.

She wrote about greeting her uncle upon his return.

Her letter:

"As we left the Milwaukee Road Depot, Uncle Ferd spotted a veritable 'gem' of a chunk on a 1939 LaSalle just across Washington Avenue. It was a shiny black pearl of at least 15 stone. Uncle Ferd's eyes rolled back in his head—a bit of saliva oozed from his lips (freezing instantly), and he took off after that chunk, unmindful of the oncoming traffic.

"Shouting phrases like a Karate Master and using amazing speed and agility, he zig-zagged through cars and launched a devastating centrifugal spinning kick.

"But it was 20 below and I had forgotten to warn Uncle Ferd about the hazards of Minnesota winters. That chunk never budged, and there stood Uncle Ferd—vibrating like a tuning fork. He was never able to kick again after that."

I don't know how many years we milked the chunk kicking craze. But I still meet people who ask, "Kicked any good chunks lately?" Randy says he meets the same fans even during his retirement in Florida. Think of us the next time you dispatch a good chunk.

**DAGMAR**, allowing **Howard Viken**
to play male chauvinist.

Top: Olympic Gold Medalist **Dorothy Hamill (Dick Chapman's** secret heartthrob). The skating star is even cuter in person.

Below: At St. Paul's Winter Carnival Parade, **Bob De Haven** and **Sherman Edwards** flanking **Johnny Carson.**

# GUESTS

Celebrities always are stalked by media outlets. Authors, stars, television standouts, political and sports luminaries.

During my years at WCCO Radio I've seen many stream through from the somewhat famous to the super-famous. We've interviewed the likes of Heavyweight Champ Muhammed Ali, film legend Sophia Loren, the incomparable Bob Hope, Carmel Quinn, Fran Allison and a rising young comic named Johnny Carson (not many knew him at the time.)

In the mid-1960s WCCO Radio hooked up with the Mendota Heights Supper Club called "Diamond Jim's" to get double duty out of show stars they brought in for special appearances. These artists doubled their income by performing nightly at the bistro and appearing daily on WCCO.

It was fascinating to watch how well these show biz veterans related to the local talent. Homer and Jethro, Morey Amsterdam, Louis Nye, Carmel Quinn, Henny Youngman, Jaye P. Morgan, Pat Butram—to a person, they enjoyed appearing with the likes of Boone, Erickson, Viken, DeHaven, all of us.

People under 30 probably won't remember Homer and Jethro. Picking on banjoes and mandolins, they had one of the freshest country and western comedy routines in the country. And they were great ad-libbers.

Pat Butram (Gene Autry's cowboy movie sidekick) went on to some meatier roles. Butram was no slouch as a comic ad-libber, either, and he was a wealth of inside Hollywood dirt.

He told of Autry almost laughing himself into apoplexy when told that his movie rival Roy Rogers had his horse, "Trigger," stuffed when the old nag died.

Butram also described Frank Sinatra as suffering from a "migraine hard-on."

Morey Amsterdam was a veteran comic, perhaps best remembered as the colleague on the Dick Van Dyke Show who swapped one-liners with Mary Tyler Moore.

Morey made history alongside myself, Paul Giel and 'CCO Promotion Director Rob Brown. It was the time when snowmobile madness engulfed the Upper Midwest. Rob Brown cooked up a promotion whereby the four of us would stage a short snowmobile race down the Nicollet Mall. First Morey and I on one machine, versus Paul and Rob on another. Then Morey and Rob would switch for the return lap. All of this broadcast live.

Morey Amsterdam was hilarious, donning massive ill-fitting snowmobile gear. He was dangerous at the controls—almost running over a pedestrian at 8th and Nicollet.

History was made because the Nicollet Mall was not yet open. Construction had just been completed, but the official opening and ribbon cutting was a day away. It was a minor detail that Rob had missed as he set up the stunt.

The fact is, Morey Amsterdam, Paul Giel, Dick Chapman and Rob Brown drove the first vehicles on the Nicollet Mall. It was a snowmobile exclusive—and there was Hell to pay to the Chamber of Commerce and City Council.

I remember other celebrity guests.

Joan Fontaine was a royal pain in the ass.

She treated Charlie Boone and myself as necessary dirt that she was forced to appear with for an interview she didn't want to do anyway. She kept arguing with her agent that Barbra Streisand's current hit "People" didn't make sense and was a lousy song. "People" became a platinum seller.

Big-Time Broadway Producer David Merrick was another pain in the ass.

He was accompanied by an entourage of yes-men, swirling around him like drones attending the queen bee. Charlie and I were about to hit the air when Merrick learned we planned to accept calls from listeners. Merrick whispered to an aide. The aide informed us that, "Mr. Merrick does not accept questions from listeners."

We explained that it was the basic format of the show.

Again a muffled conference (apparently Merrick never spoke directly to anyone), and the aide said listener call-ins were out of the question.

Charlie Boone summarily dismissed him. I gotta hand it to Charlie. He by-passed the aide, speaking directly to Merrick, and said,"No listener participation—no broadcast."

Merrick and entourage packed up and left.

We did the show after explaining that the famous Mr. Merrick wouldn't talk with common folk. To Hell with whatever traveling production he was in town to promote. I hadn't felt that good in a long time. Thanks, Charlie.

Movie Producer Otto Preminger was a delight. With his cleanly shaved head he'd look at me with those haunting eyes and say, "Shave your head! You're going bald anyway—face it—a shaved head is much neater." I should have listened to him. Yul Brynner and Telly Savalas didn't do too bad.

Broadway Musical Superstar Carol Channing may be one of the warmest and most delightful entertainers I've ever met. She just bubbles life and enthusiasm. When she debuted in "Hello, Dolly," she did a bump and grind dance routine that forced management to cordon off the first two rows of theater seats.

Roger Erickson used to write her into the Boone-Erickson skits whenever she was in town. She'd revel in doing the part.

Once she had just returned from Russia. Tim Russell called into the studio mimicking President Reagan who was about to visit Moscow. (Russell did a great Reagan and he sounds more like George Burns than Burns himself.)

As Reagan, he asked Carol Channing's advice as to how to conduct himself. What followed, totally unscripted, was some of the funniest and freshest radio you'll ever hear. Russell's voices are the best. Channing's comedy is tremendous.

Mickey Rooney was groovy. I had to shake his hand. Then, like an idiot, I told him how I enjoyed the "Andy Rooney" movies. Mickey played "Andy Hardy" not "Rooney." Apparently I'm not the only person to make that slip. Mickey, smilingly, threatened to punch me out.

I couldn't believe how short Kirk Douglas was. All those pictures with flexing muscles and swashbuckling stunts. He had a nicely proportioned body, but he didn't reach five-foot-six. Alan Ladd was supposed to have been the same way. They put him on a step-stool for love scenes with his leading ladies.

The beauteous Brooke Shields, on the other hand, is surprisingly large. She's a six-footer—perfectly put together—looks as I've always felt an Amazon woman warrior would look.

Ice skating star Dorothy Hamill is cute as a bug's ear—one of those rarities who look better in person than on TV.

Ditto for TV's Phyllis George. Her complexion is true peaches and cream, and her face pertly angelic.

The one-liner King, Henny Youngman, was quicker than a whip. He was approached by an admiring 'CCO-staff member (a woman of some years) who gushed, "Mr. Youngman, I've been here for 30 years."

His reply, "Whatsamatter, couldn't you get a cab?"

Dagmar was dynamite! I've written about her in the chapter focused on Ray Christensen.

There were many stars. Most were a pleasure to meet.

**DICK CHAPMAN**
Official portrait as President of the Minnesota Press Club.

# CHAPPY

What about Dick Chapman, the guy who's writing this epistle?

Well, I'm a newsman. Proud of it. If I'm cut, I bleed news. I'll go to my grave defending the profession of Journalism. I'm hurt by the recent public antipathy toward the news media. I admit there have been abuses, but I've known too many giants in the profession to lambaste all reporters. It's as true today as it was when Thomas Jefferson said, "There can be no freedom or democracy without a free press."

Many times I've heard, "Your job must be exciting."

It's like most other jobs, which means it can be boring, tiresome, even drudgery at times. But yes, there are those exciting times. There are those hilarious events. There are times of peril. There are times of sadness. In this chapter, I'll pick out a few from a career of more than 45 years.

I got bit by the news bug in high school, writing for the school paper. I got bit by broadcasting when a Kansas City disc jockey invited teens to guest on his record show.

What a kick! Talk into this microphone and reach all those people.

I graduated from high school at age 16, thanks to promotions during elementary school. Promotions should never be allowed. I think it advances the kids too quickly. I can say that, looking back. At the time I thought I was hot stuff.

It was 1946, and I had been offered a football scholarship at the

University of Missouri. In those days that was nothing more than books and tuition, food at the training table for cheap, and a 50 cent an hour job in the University's Physical Ed. Department. I was torn between that and the Marine Corps. The G-I Bill was still available.

It all became a moot point when a hit-and-run driver clobbered me, and cost me my left leg. They never caught the guy.

To Mizzou's credit, they honored the scholarship that first year. One of my jobs was to run phone lines for Missouri's famed coach Don Faurot, inventor of the Split-T formation. That afforded me the thrill of following the line of scrimmage during the Missouri-SMU game and watch one of the great super stars of the game, SMU's Doak Walker. Doak was so good, I never saw him off his feet during that game except when he wanted to be, like on a sensational, diving, pass catch for a TD.

After that first year, I worked my way through college. File clerk for the IRS one summer; house painter another. But best of all, I got a job washing dishes during the school year at Christian College, an all-girl school. Work one meal and eat three meals a day. It beat the hell out of Columbia, Missouri's going student wage of 50 cents per hour. I was able to augment that with my first broadcast job as a disc jockey on 500-watt KFRU. Yep, 50 cents an hour.

But I worked my way into the first talent fee of my career as host of "Disc Derby," a mail request record show from 11 to midnight five days a week. For processing the mail and spinning the wax, I earned 75 cents for that particular hour. Hey, that worked out to an extra $1.25 per week.

I squeezed in some amateur theater at Christian College and the other all-girl's school, Stephens College. They needed men for male roles. I had a bit part in a play starring George C. Scott, a Missouri U. grad who went on to Oscar heights. George C. Scott went out for some beers with a few of us after rehearsals. Believe me, he was just as wild and unpredictable in those days as he became known to be later. I wasn't at all surprised when he refused to show up for his Oscar for the movie "Patton." My college roommate was Robert Loggia, another thespian who's done quite well (Oscar nomination for "Razor's Edge").

Let's just say my acting career was up and down—maybe checkered is a better description.

There was my role in George Kaufman's "Butter and Egg Man" as a chain-smoking, wise-cracking theatrical producer. We did it "in the round"—the audience surrounding the stage. My character's chain-smoking requirement kept me lighting up constantly. As I fumbled for my lighter in the third act, a guy in the front row leaned on stage to light my cigarette for me. Unfortunately, it drew the best laugh of the lousy play.

I'll never forget dress rehearsal before a full audience for "The Lady's Not for Burning."

The leading lady faints in the third act, whereupon I make a quick two-step move and catch her. I was a tad far away, and I missed her. It was gruesome the way she hit the floor. During the regular run of the play, I kept inching closer like a baserunner leading off first base, and she did the slowest collapse you've ever seen. It was awful.

I decided early on I was not cut out for the theater, let alone the "Silver Screen." Besides, who wants to study acting at Missouri U. Their drama department actually flunked a young playwright named Tennessee Williams. (It's true!)

I squeezed out of college with a Bachelor of Journalism, a Bachelor of Arts in Creative Writing and 12 hours as an upper grad, but one thesis short of a Master's Degree. Finances finally caught up with me. It was time to earn money.

## HIGH (AND DRY) IN ODESSA

Money in that first job was $62.50 a week at KCBD in Lubbock, Texas. What a shock for a beer lover like myself to discover Lubbock was a dry town.

They had a 3.2 beer proposal on the ballot during the Eisenhower election in 1952. Bootleggers and Southern Baptist Ministers teamed up to defeat it 3 to 1.

Hispanic bigotry in Lubbock was incredible. There were no blacks to discriminate against, so they took it out on the sizeable Mexican population.

Windows had tongue-in-groove sills to keep out the dust. That worked somewhat when the "red dusters" blew in, but even the natives ran for cover when the mysterious "black dusters" rolled up. Day turned to night, and no one knows to this day where the black dust comes from.

KCBD was 1590 on the dial. Some radios didn't have dials that went that high.

My days at KCBD were not what you would call exciting. Except for an incredible incident that thrust me into the art of play-by-play.

I was assigned as a color and commercial man with the station's long-time sports announcer. We did Lubbock High School and Texas Tech University football. In those days, the high school team could beat Texas Tech. They had a lot of talent—one high school for a town of ninety thousand. That year the Lubbock High School Hubbers won the Texas State Championship in a game at the Cotton Bowl on New Year's Eve day.

One game on that championship road took us to Odessa, Texas— another powerhouse. But an untimely fire had damaged the press box, so we were forced to work at the top of the stands across the field. No press box. No tables or chairs. Just stand up there with yoke microphones and earphones, and hold your copy in your hands.

To start the second half, Odessa went three downs and punted. A Lubbock speedster fielded the punt and returned it 45 yards nearly for a score. I'm straining to see over the screaming crowd, all on their feet and waving their arms. Suddenly, I can't hear my play-by-play colleague in my headset. I turn. He's not standing beside me. He had fallen off the back of the stands. I spotted him on hands and knees on the ground below. His microphone and headset dangled in mid air.

What was I to do? It was a pretty good drop. I had no idea of his injuries and I knew his family was listening. I simply took over the play-by-play without reference to the mishap.

It took quite some time for him to return and renew his play-by-play. We joked only lightly about his fall. He was hurting pretty much—two small wrist fractures and a dislocated kneecap. Looking back, I know it could have been fatal had he not turned a half-gainer in his plunge, landing on his hands and knees. That was my inauguration to sports play-by-play. It would come in handy in later years.

I was not anxious to stick around dry, dusty, bigoted Lubbock, Texas, for $62.50 a week.

### CAPITAL TIMES IN THE CAPITOL

I moved to KWOS in Jefferson City, Missouri for $75.00 a week.

It was one of my smartest moves ever. I was named News Director. That meant the plum newscasts mixed in with disc-jockeying, copy-writing, control operations, transmitter readings, sales pitches, and floor-sweeping. I mean, you do it all in a 250-watt station. I was dynamite playing hillbilly music on "The Dinnerbell Roundup" every noontime. The commercials taught me about Aureomicin and "Pig Mama Feeds" from Checkerboard Square in St. Louis.

But Jefferson City is the state capital. My news duties provided five years of invaluable experience covering the legislature, the Governor's office, all the workings of state governnment and the high-powered machine politics in vogue at the time. I was privileged to work with and learn from veteran reporters from major newspapers in St. Louis and Kansas City.

When is the job exciting? When you get to break news that newly-elected Governor Blair refuses to move into his mansion because it's a run-down dump. When you've got exclusive live coverage of the 1954 Missouri State Prison riot—millions in fire damage—dozens of dead convicts—bullets whizzing over your head.

## MISSOURI PRISON RIOTS

That night began with a phone call I received from an assistant warden. He wanted my station to broadcast a call for all off-duty guards to report to work. He refused to explain initially, but he happened to be a friend. I coaxed it out of him that a full-scale riot had erupted. He'd been holding back for fear of panicking the public. Dumb luck, again, that the warden was a friend. The prison was a mere four blocks away. When I arrived, half a dozen of the main buildings were spewing towering flames into the evening sky. All inmates were out of their cells, most of them rampaging in the exercise yard.

The only thing keeping them inside was a group of about a dozen highway patrol troopers scattered around the walls with shotguns. I was an eye witness when inmates ignored bullhorn commands to vacate the yard, and the troopers opened up. Dozens were cut down.

I managed one report from a phone in the yard's main guard tower before the line went dead.

At one point during the incredible night, I followed a trail of blood down a corridor through the "roundgate," the double barred main entrance to the prison's heart.

Another time, when reinforcements had bolstered the troopers, I had to dive for cover. A free-roaming inmate had smashed a cellblock window, and a nearby trooper simply sprayed the side of the building with a machine gun. Bullets ricocheted everywhere. It caused my only injury. I had to sprawl amid a mass of broken glass, suffering minor cuts that could be treated without stitches.

The rest of the nation's media had to rely on me and my little station. Dumb luck again—the right place at the right time.

For a young man from a 250-watt station to win the Sigma Delta Chi (Society of Professional Journalists) National Award—well, it's gratifying to say the least.

It was also exciting to uncover the reasons for the riot. I found an informant—a fired prison guard—who divulged nightmarish prison conditions, including corporal punishment and rancid food.

Our broadcast of these allegations triggered a second riot, and the then-Governor, Phil M. Donnelly, accused my station, and me personally, of being responsible for the flare-up. Bless my management for standing by me. A subsequent investigation by a special commission substantiated all our charges, and launched a clean-up of prison abuses. Gov. Donnelly and I never got along too well anyway.

A murder occurred during that riot. Thirteen hardened inmates broke into C-block (Death Row) where wardens had incarcerated two inmate "stool pigeons" for their own safety. One was slaughtered. The other escaped only by jamming his cell lock with pieces broken from his pocket comb. Even then, he had to use a cell stool to ward off knives taped to broomsticks.

## PROTECTED BY THE FLAG

My friendship with a judge allowed me a coup during the trial of these 13 inmates. I was allowed to place a live microphone into his courtroom—a first in Missouri history, and one of the first live courtroom broadcasts in the nation.

Therein lies another yarn.

My friend, the judge, insisted that my microphone not disrupt the decorum of the court. So I installed a fixed-gain amplifier behind the judge's bench, draped the microphone wire over a partition and concealed the microphone in the furls of an American Flag just two feet from the court reporter's ear. I figured if the court reporter couldn't hear the proceedings nobody could.

At the ensuing trials, the defense for one inmate requested, and was granted, a change of venue against my friend the judge. It didn't mean moving the trial. It meant replacing the judge in the same courtroom. My judge warned me that his permission for live broadcast would not necessarily continue under the new judge. Sure enough, the first day the new judge presided, he confiscated my tape recorder (carried as a back-up).

But he was unaware of the live microphone. I was afraid to tell him. Besides it was a critical point in the trial, and I couldn't leave—couldn't even alert my station to cease the live broadcast.

Would you believe this judge never learned that his trial was being broadcast live? When the day was over, I'm stuck with a hidden microphone in the court. We spirited it out of there after midnight with the cooperation of some courthouse cronies of mine. I asked my Capitol Press Corps buddies what penalty I could draw for contempt of court. One merely pointed to a picture on the Capitol Press Room wall—a picture I had overlooked. It was a picture of Kansas City Star Capitol Correspondent

Lew Larkin, seated at his portable typewriter, but behind bars in the Cole County jail. Ah, youth.

## TV TRIALS AND TRIUMPHS

During my years in Jefferson City, my company received a license for a television station, and I became its first news director. What an experience! I was a one-man staff. There was no video tape back then. With one 16-millimeter Bell and Howell wind-up camera, I'd shoot film, develop it, edit it, write the accompanying script and then deliver it on the air. That was while continuing my radio duties. Ah, youth is grand.

A spectacular fire occurred at the state mental hospital in nearby Fulton, Missouri. I had a light bar and located a live electrical outlet so I could film firefighters chopping through the roof of a burning building. I was up there with them, and got a sensational shot of a fireman almost falling to his death as he tried to shinny across a ladder braced between two eaves.

Eager to hurry the film back, I started to leave. The firefighters wouldn't let me. They needed my lights. Apparently I'd lucked into the only live AC outlet. I left the light bar with them and hurried my camera and film away. I never got the lights back. My boss almost took the cost out of my pay.

The aforementioned 16-millimeter camera had a single one-inch lens with accompanying tiny viewfinder. The viewfinder played a big part when I hastened to the Lake of the Ozarks where a deep sea diver was investigating a possible tragedy.

A restaurant waitress had been missing for weeks when someone reported an oil slick in ninety-foot deep water near Bagnell Dam. Scrape marks were discovered at a nearby scenic overlook, suggesting a car might have gone into the lake. The depth required a professional from St. Louis using the full diving suit with the old-fashioned steel ball helmet.

No one knew what he'd find. I'm on a nearby boat as the diver communicated with his own dive boat. The crew shouted to me, "He's found a car!"

Poised with my one-inch lens, I started shooting as the bubbles increased. Timing was perfect. The helmet broke the water just after I started rolling (remember this was just a camera you had to wind up).

Little did we know, he had not only found the car—but the waitress's body in it—and he brought the body up on that first dive. Squinting through that tiny viewfinder, I continued filming as he flung the corpse on deck. It was rigor-mortised in a sitting position which later confirmed that the poor lady had committed suicide by driving her car off the ledge.

What I couldn't see well was her face, as the body rolled on its side staring directly at my camera.

I discovered how ghastly the shot was after rushing back to soup the film. One eye was missing. Much of the flesh had been eaten away by whatever frequents the lake depths. It didn't look bad in the viewfinder, but blown up to screen size it was right out of a horror movie.

Deadline was at hand. I had no time to edit. This was a 6 p.m. suppertime newscast. What could I do? I ran to master control and told my technicians to go to black just as the body starts to roll on its side. The scoop shot was too good to waste. I just didn't want that face on the screen.

You guessed it! They didn't fade to black in time! Viewers enjoying dinner all across central Missouri were treated to something extra on the menu. Phone call complaints—Oh, yeah! I thought the switchboard would overload.

## AN EXECUTION

Carl Austin Hall and Bonnie Brown Heady were two misfits, alcoholic dregs of society, who kidnapped and murdered Bobby Greenlease, the young son of a Kansas City Cadillac dealer.

They collected a whopping half-million dollar ransom even after the boy was dead.

After capture and conviction, they were sentenced to the Missouri gas chamber, the only such facility in the nation capable of a side-by-side double execution.

Their arrival at the prison was cloaked in secrecy.

Not when you've got years of inside connections as did I and the other members of the Capitol Hill Press Corps. Plenty of reporters were there when the two arrived. I, however, had the only tape recorder.

In the quick rush from squad cars to the prison entrance I managed to tape Bonny Brown Heady remarking that it was cold, and could she borrow someone's coat. Not much, but better than nothing from a person so notorious, who would never be heard in public again.

With the scoop adrenalin flowing again I was devasated back at the studio to learn the cold had affected my recorder. The speed was off. Bonnie Brown Heady's voice was reproduced too fast. It was like she'd taken Helium. I had to get my scoop on the air.

Believe it or not, I used the eraser at the tip of a pencil to press against the tape recorder's drive wheel, thereby slowing it to the proper speed for rebroadcast.

## BLAIR AND BLARING

The aforementioned Missouri Gov. Blair was one of a kind. He was known affectionately among his constituents as Jim Tom Blair. He was a native of Jefferson City, the state capital. He was a product of what was a solid Democratic political machine (long since eroded). He was an accomplished politician and administrator. He loved what he called "bourbon and branch water."

When first elected as Governor, he astounded everyone by refusing to move into the Governor's mansion. He called it a run-down dump. He insisted on living in his own rather modest home, unless the legislature provided funds for long-overdue renovations at the mansion.

This allowed all of us in the Capitol City Press Corps (a grandiose title we gave ourselves) to milk the story as one of our better features.

The on going feud between the Governor and legislators drew national attention. I remember earning extra network money by filming and taping the Governor as he led us through the mansion, pointing out the many flaws. Externally, the mansion was imposing, but inside, indeed, there were problems. The roof leaked. A third floor shower had only enough water pressure to provide a dribble of water. Some toilets didn't flush properly. The wiring was faulty—not even up to code in some rooms. But worst of all was the china and silverware service. There weren't enough matching pieces to stage a formal state dinner. I believe some place settings numbered less than eight.

It made for great press over a number of weeks, and Jim Tom Blair reveled in the pressure he could place on his lawmakers. Ultimately, they had to give in, but it took time.

During that time, the Governor's birthday rolled around.

The Capitol City Press Corps enjoyed great rapport with Gov. Blair so we came up with the idea of throwing him a birthday party—at the mansion.

The Governor thought it a great idea. He even popped for the food and drink. (We knew he would.) Then we surprised him. For birthday gifts each of us brought a (cheap) place setting—a knife, fork, spoon, dishes, saucers, and cups—it doubled him over.

The night of the party got a bit out of hand. The food and drink flowed like that at a medieval feast. A few of us wandered to the nearby Capitol building itself, and flew paper airplanes from inside the top of the dome. How we got by security people is probably explained by the fact the Governor was with us.

One reporter from the Daily Capitol News fancied himself as a rising trumpet player. He hadn't risen very far yet, but he always kept his horn along with him. Naturally, he drug it out to practice that memorable night, and somewhere on either side of midnight he decided to practice on the front porch of the mansion, just outside the main entrance.

Well, there were some fancy homes and apartments just across the street. The residents therein didn't appreciate the sound of that trumpet during their sleeping hours. They called the cops.

The image of what followed is forever engraved in my mind. Two squad cars screeched up in front of the Governor's mansion as my newspaper colleague blared away on his trumpet. Spotlights from both squad cars lit up my friend who was already lit. Officers jumped from the cars. Because of the spotlights, I'll never know if they had drawn their weapons.

At that very moment, Governor Blair emerged from the mansion and draped his arm across the shoulders of our trumpet-playing buddy.

The officers hadn't had time even to speak. So help me—they merely turned off the spotlights, shrugged their shoulders, and drove away.

Those are just some of the highlights during my five-year stint in Missouri's Capital. Suffice it to say, it was worth more than the five years in Journalism school and a year in the Texas Panhandle. You can't buy that kind of training. You can't rub elbows with such great reporters and news sources. If I had any advice to a cub reporter, it would be: try to get a job in a state capital—any state capital.

## ON TO 'CCO-LAND

My ego started getting the best of me. I was a big fish in a little pond. I accepted a job at WCCO Radio in June of 1957. It was a 50,000-watt clear channel giant. Besides it was in Minnesota where I had spent a couple of summers discovering the thrills of angling for walleyes and northerns, far more exotic than the bass, panfish, catfish and carp of the Missouri Ozarks.

But my first duties were quite a comedown. WCCO Radio still suffered from "networkitis," a throwback from the days CBS owned and operated 'CCO. Announcers were all golden-throated, but stiff and impersonal. (Cedric Adams was the only exception.) Newswriters like me wrote copy for other people. We never got on the air for scheduled newscasts. It was agony for a guy used to writing and delivering his own material.

My first 'CCO scoop came as I toiled alone one weekend. A police officer called with a request to try to locate friends or relatives of one Wilbur Foshay. It seems Mr. Foshay had died, alone and penniless, as he slept in a Minneapolis flophouse.

To a newcomer, the first thing noticeable in Minneapolis was this single oddly-shaped skyscraper, emblazoned with the word "FOSHAY."

So I asked the officer, "Any relation to the Foshay Tower Foshay?"

"I dunno," said the cop. "Could be."

There was no foul play, Wilbur Foshay just up and died in his sleep, the clothes on his back his only possessions.

A few phone calls and some digging revealed that it was the once flamboyant Wilbur Foshay who had built a multi-million dollar paper empire and erected what was then the tallest skyscraper west of Chicago. He was the man who commissioned March King John Phillip Sousa to write "The Foshay Tower March" and then hire Sousa and his 100-member band to perform at the building's dedication. He was the man who invited Presidents, Kings, Queens, Sultans and Rajahs to that same dedication, showering them with gold watches and memorabilia. He was the man sent to prison for fraud when his financial empire collapsed—a trial some still think was a political frame-up.

At any rate, my naivete produced the scoop. Similar try-to-locate calls to the press and other media types fell on deaf ears. Everyone but me missed the Foshay connection and aired the message routinely.

My scoop ran on Saturday and Sunday. The StarTribune didn't catch up until Monday afternoon. You gotta be lucky to get scoops.

The great poet, Bobby Burns, should have written: "O, the Power the gift Hae gae us to see oursilthes in time ahead, sted that behind us."

Had Burns (my favorite) written that, perhaps I wouldn't have made such a lousy decision. (Terrible pun, re: "Ode to a Louse.")

It was one of my earliest mundane assignments. As a 'CCO rookie I was sent to cover a news conference where a new company called Control Data was to unveil its first computer.

The Control Data people were rebels who jumped from the National Cash Register Company (a few from IBM) to take a gamble on this new venture.

The assignment didn't seem earth-shaking to me, but as Control Data introduced the computer and described its capabilities, my interest grew. The new computer had been sold to the U.S. Navy for one million dollars. My interest really grew when told the Navy had ordered nine more.

One Control Data Vice President told me, "Our stock is selling for one dollar a share. You'd be smart to buy some."

As green as I was regarding the computer field, I still was smart enough at least to consider such an investment.

But at the time I was struggling to pay the rent. Had I been able to scrape up an extra one or two hundred dollars, I'm sure I would have. At the time I had $7.87 in my pocket. I could imagine my wife's reaction if I had come home to tell her I'd bought some stock in a fledgling company.

Control Data's meteoric rise started the moment after I left the news conference. I could have doubled or tripled my investment in less than one week. I don't even want to think about the possible earnings through the years. "O, the power the gift Hae gae us!"

One of my career scoops was another perfect example of being in the right place at the right time. All the experience and preparation in the world can't make up for just plain luck.

### GITCHI GUMEE GOOF-UPS

I was sent to Duluth-Superior to cover the Grand Opening and Dedication of the Twin Ports Seaway Facility, a multi-million dollar construction at the very end of the Great Lakes new connection to the oceans of the world. When the Soo Locks were completed, Washington D.C. commissioned an armada of naval vessels to inaugurate the new system with stops by various ships at major ports throughout the Great Lakes. Some of the ports hosted battleships and cruisers. Duluth-Superior was geared up to welcome a destroyer and two submarines.

The big Gala was timed for the three vessels to enter the Twin Ports harbor beneath Duluth's famous "Lift Bridge" at precisely 8 a.m. on Saturday. Thousands could be seated ashore to witness and cheer the dramatic event, and believe me, thousands turned out on a beautiful day.

I was determined to wangle myself aboard the destroyer prior to arrival with the hopes of doing a live broadcast from the ship itself, not a simple task in this man's Navy.

I spent the entire prior evening searching for ways to do this. The only media boat was primarily designed for photographers. It was to await the fleet's arrival inside the harbor.

I had all but given up when I lucked into the information that a small Coast Guard cutter was going out early to meet the destroyer. The purpose—so help me God—was to carry a delegation of four from the local USO, sent to invite the crews to a Saturday night dance. I talked myself aboard.

This Coast Guard "cutter" was nothing more than a 20-some-foot power boat. The big lake was relatively calm, which means three to four foot swells. Departing at dawn, we were out quite a few miles before encountering the destroyer traveling at about half speed.

I couldn't believe it when the guardsmen pulled alongside, matched the destroyer's speed, and indicated the only way aboard was for us to jump from the Coast Guard craft to a flexible step ladder hanging amidship. In those swells, and at that speed, it was hairy to say the least.  One of the USO people, a woman, nearly missed. Had that happened, it could have been fatal. I was lugging a tape recorder and it took all my courage to make that jump. But we succeeded.

Deadline was approaching and I grabbed the first officer I could spot with gold on his visor and indicated my haste to deliver a live radio broadcast. He said, "Follow me!"

Typical of some officers, he didn't know much about anything. He took me to the destroyer's "radio shack" where two enlisted swabbies were manning the radio gear. After explaining my request, these two guys rolled their eyes and politely told the officer it couldn't be done from there. One suggested, again politely, that I be taken to the bridge.

These communication guys knew that the destroyer had just been fitted with a new ship-to-shore telephone linked to the Great Lakes network.

Arriving on the bridge, I couldn't help but wonder where this officer's brains were, because there, hanging on the wall, was a shiny blue telephone. It was the only thing of color against a bridge that was otherwise totally white. You couldn't miss it. It stood out like a sore thumb.

I was introduced to the flotilla Commodore (an honorary position) and to the actual destroyer Captain, and they bent over backwards to assist me. This, after all, was a Navy public relations cruise.

The connection back to WCCO Radio was perfect—crystal clear. I was delighted—broadcasting live from the destroyer's bridge—interviewing both the Captain and Commodore. After the broadcast, all hell broke loose!

The first thing that went wrong involved the fire hoses. Two powerful hoses were pumping water into the air at Duluth's famed "lift bridge," forming a dazzling water arch. The sun-bathed crowd was cheering. The bands were playing. The destroyer's crew was turned out aforedeck in full parade dress, standing at attention.

The plan, obviously, was to shut down the hoses as the destroyer entered the narrow harbor entrance.

Only one of the hoses got turned off! The other hose mowed down the sailors on deck like bowling pins. Embarrassing! Of course! But hilarious, nonetheless. To the crew's credit, they had the mops out instantly and returned to attention quickly, albeit a bit drippy.

Then the near disaster occurred.

Sweeping in off the middle of Lake Superior came four jet fighters—Delta Daggers—in tight formation and perhaps five hundred feet high. It was to be a surprise salute from the Duluth Air National Guard Base. They timed it perfectly, roaring over at top speed.

But right in their flight path was a single engine private plane. It looked like not much more than a Piper Cub to me.

The four jets broke formation and streaked by the little aircraft on all sides. It seemed to shudder in mid-air.

Officers on the bridge shouted, "Did you see that? How close was that? How did they miss him? Holy Mackerel!" It was pandemonium.

The only other reporter aboard was a newspaperman from the Duluth Herald Tribune who had the foresight to board the destroyer back in Chicago. We compared notes on what we had just witnessed and decided that it was inches from being a terrible disaster. How many could have been killed? The huge crowd itself would have been showered with wreckage.

Now comes my dumb luck again. The media boat with all the photographers was on the wrong side of the destroyer and too close. No one aboard saw what we saw from the destroyer's bridge. I had my scoop. So did the reporter from Duluth, but he didn't publish until the next morning.

I worked the story to death in my reports all day long, until my boss, Jim Bormann, asked me to get some confirmation. He said, "Nobody else has the story. I'm getting calls from the Network, the AP, UP, even the New York Times."

"Jim," I said, "I saw it with my own eyes!"

He said, "I don't give a damn, call the Air National Guard, call the Navy, call somebody to corroborate your story."

Thanks a lot, boss. It wasn't that easy. I spent the entire day only to discover that somebody had put the lid on what had happened. The Air National Guard didn't know what I was talking about. The Navy—I couldn't even find my shipmates from the bridge. Time to get lucky again.

An old friend from my Missouri days, Gordon Slovut, was working for the Duluth Herald Tribune. He went on to a bigger career with the Minneapolis StarTribune. Gordy also happened to be a member of the Duluth Air National Guard. To make a long story short, he knew the pilots of the four-jet fly-over, and subtly introduced me to the lead pilot that evening in a Duluth supper club. We chatted idly over a beer and I casually asked "How close was that today?"

The pilot gushed forth as though he couldn't contain himself any longer. He said, "It was so close, I don't know if I went under him or over him!" He added, "When I saw him, I yelled "break," and looked out to see that my wing man was already gone."

It turned out that the small aircraft had been hired by a free-lance photographer from Omaha, and had flown directly to Minnesota—unaware that he was entering restricted airspace. Again, as luck would have it, that same free-lancer was at the same supper club. He told me, "I thought the wings were going to come off. You couldn't believe the noise. Only my laundromat will know how scared I was!"

I had my confirmation, but it wasn't needed. The Sunday morning edition of the Duluth Herald Tribune carried the story under a banner headline: "NEAR TRAGEDY—MID AIR COLLISION AVERTED!"

### WHAT'S IN A NAME?

I also lucked into an exclusive interview with a teen-age lad from near Hastings, Minnesota. He was a survivor of a fiery jet-bomber crash that slammed into his family's farm.

The jet—on a routine mid-air refueling mission—exploded aloft and spiraled to the ground. Only one parachuting crewmember survived. The farm house was demolished. There were serious burns to the occupants. The boy I interviewed was wrapped in bandages from head to foot.

I couldn't believe the cooperation I received from hospital administrators. The hospital head marched me right into the patient's room, just an hour or two after treatment.

Luck! The adminstrator remarked as we left, "You know your Mr. Ridder is on our Board of Directors!" Bernie Ridder, President of the St. Paul Pioneer Press and Dispatch, was also President of Midwest Communications—holding company of WCCO Radio and TV. I don't think Bernie ever knew he helped me get the sensational interview.

## PRINCE OF NORWAY

During Minnesota's celebration of the 100th anniversary of statehood, I teamed with Jerry Roshholt to broadcast live descriptions of, of all things, the Centennial Parade. I thought that stuff went out with the Bob and Ray comedy team.

I was also assigned to cover the airport arrival of the Prince of Norway. We were all set up with a 'CCO van and a live microphone on the roof. At the last moment, authorities changed the airport berth of the airplane—at least a thousand yards away.

Well, you can't just break down and move in seconds. So there I stood on the van's roof—wind tossing my hair, barely able to see anything—and made the whole thing up. I ad-libbed the Prince's arrival from his smile and clothing, to an imaginary little girl handing him flowers. Turned out there *was* a little girl who did just that, but I couldn't see her. Ah, youth.

## JFK

The job becomes exciting when you cover a rising political rocket like John F. Kennedy. I did just that when Kennedy locked horns with Minnesota's Senator Hubert Humphrey during Wisconsin's primary campaign.

I chased both those guys all over Wisconsin in a 1956 'CCO Chevy station wagon in bad need of repair. Kennedy (always accompanied by what we called the "Irish Mafia") roared from small town to small town never acknowledging a speed limit. It was all I could do in that 6-cylinder crate to keep up.

I'll never forget whizzing through a 35-mile-an-hour posted stretch near a small town school. The Kennedy caravan was doing perhaps 75 mph. School zone lights were flashing for God's sake! And worse yet, classes had just let out, and the shoulder of the highway was loaded with school kids. Visions of newspaper headlines flashed through my head:

"PRESIDENTIAL CANDIDATE'S CAR KILLS SEVEN
YOUNGSTERS!"

Or:

"KENNEDY KILLS KIDS!"

I like to believe that the Senator from Massachusetts was pre-occupied with paper work and unaware of what his drivers were doing, but I'll never know.

It was a breakneck whirlwind campaign. The Senator pressed the flesh and repeated often, "Hello, I'm Senator Kennedy and I'm running for President."

The western portions of Wisconsin were primarily Republican. Yet, I couldn't help but notice the preponderance of women who turned out to see him—Republican women! It was sex appeal! Pure and simple. JFK had sex appeal, and I'll bet many of those Republican housewives crossed the Party line and voted for him—since it was only a primary. Some may have done the same in the general election.

That high speed caravan rolled into a consolidated high school for Eleva-Strum, Wisconsin. I chugged in, late as usual, with an excruciating urge to go to the men's room. I slipped into the school's rear doors right into the locker room behind the gym. Senator John F. Kennedy was there alone, doing his business at a urinal.

Automatically he turned, thrust out his hand and said, "Hello, I'm Senator Kennedy and I'm running for President."

I said, "For God's sake, Jack, I've been with you for three weeks, the least you can do is wash your hands!"

He quickly recognized me and broke into laughter, the most genuine laughter I'd ever heard from a normally laid back man.

Pressing my advantage, I said, "By the way—your fly is open."

Yes, there are those moments when the job is fun.

Jackie Kennedy was something—a striking beauty, but curiously not as pretty in person as in photographs. She stayed out of the limelight. Somehow I got the impression that she knew Jack's campaigners wanted her as tinsel and glitter rather than a "brainy and supportive" potential First Lady. A Hillary Clinton she was not.

I believe it's true that she had a fetish about the size of her feet—a popular rumor at the time. They *were* a bit large for a lady who was otherwize neatly proportioned. I'd notice her tuck them away during photo opportunities. She'd hide them behind table cloths or chairs.

I bring this up because of another exclusive interview I lucked into. It was in Milwaukee. The primary votes were being counted and the Kennedys were at the studios of a major TV outlet to claim victory. The win was official. I sped out of the studios for a quiet telephone, did a quick broadcast, and started back to where JFK was delivering his victory speech.

Down the deserted hallway came Jackie Kennedy. She was humming a nonsensical tune and twirling her shoes in her hand. It was as though, "Glad that's over, maybe I can relax for a while."

Suddenly I appear with an obvious tape recorder on my shoulder. She stopped and quickly shrugged back into her shoes. It wasn't that easy nor graceful. Perhaps her feet had swollen a bit. I couldn't help but notice their size.

She was graceful, however, when I whipped out a microphone and launched into an impromptu interview. It was perhaps the most anyone had gotten out of Jackie during the entire primary campaign. Just dumb luck—the right place at the right time.

### HST

And then there's Harry S. Truman and another dumb luck exclusive I managed to luck into.

After leaving the White House, Truman was invited to deliver one of the Green Foundation Lectures at tiny Westminster College in Fulton, Missouri. The College had been placed on the world map by a fellow named Winston Churchill. At one of those same lectures the former British statesman had delivered his famous "Iron Curtain" speech—lamenting what the Soviets were doing across eastern Europe.

Fulton was only 30 miles from Jefferson City where I was holding forth as News Director. I managed to convince my managment that the Truman speech warranted live coverage on our little 250-watter. Damn the expense! Let's do it!

The speech was set for noon. I'm set with a live microphone at the podium of the college's famed chapel. I also had a personal phone for cueing purposes.

Big-time press was there. But the media opted for tape and film, leaving me with the only live coverage.

At mid-morning the Atomic Energy Commission dismissed Dr. Robert Oppenheimer as a security risk. Oppenheimer was called "the Father of the Atomic Bomb." And Oppenheimer had been appointed by President Harry S. Truman.

"Security Risk!"

The word spread like wildfire. The story cried out for comment from Harry.

I asked a janitor where he thought I could find the President. He said, "He's probably walking over here from lunch right now."

I fled out the door, turned left, rounded a corner and literally bumped into Harry Truman. I mean I physically ran into him in my haste. I almost knocked him down!

We were both flustered. I blurted out, "Harry, they fired Oppenheimer!"

Truman barked, "Them dirty sons of bitches!"

I said, "I don't think I can use that, Mr. President, can you comment further?"

Whereupon he launched into an ad-lib defense of Dr. Oppenheimer, condemning the AEC, and said, "I'll stake my own career on Dr. Oppenheimer's reputation and loyalty."

With no tape recorder, all I could do was take notes furiously.

Suddenly a horde of reporters came swooping around the other side of the chapel. They descended on Mr. Truman, bombarding him with the Oppenheimer occurrence to which Truman said, "No Comment!"

Realizing what I had, I tip-toed away, re-entered the chapel, phoned my station and said, "Put me on the air instantly from the live microphone on the podium."

From there I scooped the nation while the other reporters badgered Truman outside. We carried his speech live, but he never mentioned the Oppenheimer event.

He didn't comment until the next day, delivering essentially what he blurted out to me when I ran into him 24 hours earlier.

The Associated Press, the New York Times, the St. Louis Globe Democrat, the Kansas City Star (countless others) had to credit my little 250-watt radio station when reprinting what President Truman had told me. Yes, the job can be fun and exciting sometimes.

## SOME OTHER COMMENTS

While I'm on this subject of Presidential politics, let me interject this. I've covered the head men from Harry S. Truman to Bill Clinton. I never had the opportunity to meet Dwight Eisenhower, Lyndon Johnson or Ronald Reagan, personally.

But I did one-on-one interviews three times with Richard Nixon. I have a "Nixon for President" button he gave me personally. I must say the man never looked me in the eye, and never answered a question directly. I admit, I never liked him.

I also did a one-on-one with Barry Goldwater—Mr. Conservative himself. He, unlike Nixon, always looked you in the eye and never ducked a question. I didn't vote for him, but I always liked him.

Jimmy Carter struck me as the wrong man in the wrong place at the wrong time. However, he must be credited for the Mideast Peace accords between Egypt's Anwar Sadat and Israel's Menachem Begin. Carter's wife, Rosalynn, was delightful.

George Bush drove me crazy with his phraseology and one liners. "Read my lips" is a prime example. But he's an avid angler so he's not all bad.

Bill Clinton never should have presumed he could storm into Washington D.C. and take on the establishment with his own cronies from Arkansas. I thought he was a Rhodes Scholar.

## HHH

And then there's Hubert H. Humphrey—the man who should have been President of the United States.

That sentence alone will bring his critics and enemies out of the woodwork.

I don't give a damn! The man was the closest thing to a statesman I've ever covered in our political world that gets crazier and crazier as the decades roll on.

By the time I started covering Hubert Humphrey, he was already the junior Senator from Minnesota. The senior Senator at that time was Ed Thye, a conservative Republican with long tenure. Nonetheless, few across the nation knew of Ed Thye, because this wild-eyed flaming liberal named Hubert (Horatio, of all things) Humphrey was capturing all the headlines with his outlandish proposals. Hubert H. Humphrey could orate like no one else. Sen. Thye's oratory left something to be desired.

When my profession destined that our paths would cross, I approached Hubert Humphrey with complete objectivity. I knew nothing of his Mayoralty in Minneapolis. I knew very little of his Capitol Hill record. I did know of his Civil Rights speech before the Democratic National Convention. I was aware that conservative Democrats walked out of that convention to form the Dixiecrats. I was aware that Harry Truman won the election anyway. But even I thought HHH might be a bit too liberal for the majority of Democrats or the majority of the country.

So it was that from 1957 until his death, I watched the development of a liberal politician into a man of compromise who never lost sight of what an elected official must strive for. He compromised, yes—but never renounced his Liberal philosophy—he just tempered it, to get things done.

There was no denying his ability to thrive in the power circles of Washington, D.C.

A politician—you bet he was! But, how many people react negatively to the very word "politician." Politics—bad word.

Hubert H. Humphrey never accepted that. Hubert spent his entire career boosting politics as the noblest of professions. Hubert urged everyone to get involved in running their own country, state, county or community. Hubert felt that to be selected for public service was the greatest of all compliments. He delivered a speech on the floor of his beloved Senate that brought tears to the eyes of his seasoned colleagues. He was dying. Everyone knew it. Yet Hubert delivered a sermon (if you will) chastising his counterparts to realize what an honor the Senate is, and never lose sight of why they're there.

I watched the man build a national following. He fought for the family farm against the corporate trend that was gobbling up acres. As his stature grew, he plunged into foreign policy. Do you remember his marathon session with Nikita Khrushchev inside the Kremlin?

Hubert and Nikita dropped from sight for more than 24 hours. It was scheduled to be a routine diplomatic meeting. The entire world grew curious as the hours stacked up. I remember chuckling to myself, "With Hubert's propensity to talk, and both men having to go through interpreters, it might take a week."

At any rate, it was becoming a mega-story. I got in line to interview Hubert by telephone whenever he emerged from the marathon. I hadn't moved quickly enough. WCCO Radio was placed about 35th on a list of calls waiting. The New York Times was first, followed by many other media organizations. The Minneapolis StarTribune was high on the list—fourth, I think.

Here comes my dumb luck again!

I had spent hours and lots of telephone charges talking globally to reach Hubert's hotel, only to get a disappointing spot on his waiting list. But when Hubert emerged, a bulletin flashed the information world wide, and I was prepared to wait.

Somewhere in that intricate world telephone network, somebody made a mistake. The phone rang at WCCO Radio just before our prime morning news bloc. First an operator in Rome, then another in Helsinki, finally one in Moscow. I don't know exactly which operator I was connected with (Moscow exchange or hotel), but she asked, "Minneapolis StarTribune?"

I said, "Yes!" Forgive me, Mr. Cowles! (Publisher) – My deadline was much more stringent than the newspaper's.

What followed was a terrific interview with Hubert, live from Moscow, very soon after his marathon session with Khrushchev.

Hubert and Nikita had debated everything from the arms race, to the cold war, to comparisons of Communism and Capitalism. They just kept talking—sometimes arguing—right through several meals. Neither man slept. One humorous exchange came as Khrushchev spoke of Communism as it was being practiced in the People's Republic of China.

Khrushchev didn't think much of China's commune system—harsh little cells of citizens barely eking out a living, and dotted across the vast country. Hubert quoted Khrushchev as saying, "We learned long ago that that doesn't work. In Russia today we offer incentives for improved productivity. We give bonuses to the better workers." Hubert replied, "Excuse me, Mr. Chairman, but that sounds like Capitalism to me."

Khrushchev said, "Call it what you want. We know what works!"

As Vice President, Hubert Humphrey had to sit on his principles and tether his tongue while President Lyndon Johnson struggled with the cancer of Viet Nam. He was fulfilling the unwritten rule of the vice presidency, hating it all the time. When Hubert Humphrey divorced America's policy of involvement in 'Nam, the American public couldn't forget his four years of silence as LBJ's Veep.

The election of 1968 we all remember as incendiary—riots in Chicago—protests everywhere.

Yet the trend of voter polls show that Hubert H. Humphrey would have won the Presidency had the campaign lasted one or two more weeks. He was climbing that fast in the surveys, and his loss was the narrowest in history.

Hubert was still a viable candidate four years later. He pulled out. He knew something no one else did. He had developed cancer.

He underwent considerable treatment before returning to the Senate. It was a triumphal return, but laden with sadness. Everyone knew he was losing his fight to the disease. I remember his floor speech well.

I was so moved by his words that day I fired off an emotional letter to him. Never mind that my profession requires political objectivity.

Hubert Humphrey died January 14, 1978. President Jimmy Carter declared National mourning and flew Hubert's body to lie in state in the nation's Capitol. It was returned quickly for the same reviewal in Minnesota's Capitol before burial in Lakewood Cemetery in Minneapolis. The funeral was attended by President Carter, Vice President Mondale, and a host of Hubert's Capitol Hill colleagues.

The speed of these events and the security required made for a monumental task of news coverage.

Oct. 26, 1977

The Hon. Hubert H. Humphrey
United States Senator
Old Senate Office Bldg.
Washington, D.C.

I listened to Charles Osgood on CBS Radio today, recapping
your return to the U.S. Senate, in Charlie's inimitable
reporting style.  It brought tears to my eyes.

I don't believe they were tears of sadness, just a welling
of warmth and strength and humanity—you have become
my champion.  God, but you're a tough old fighter.

I lost a leg to a hit-run driver at age 16, suffered an
attack of Multiple Sclerosis in prime years, and often
had the tempting impulse to look up and say, "Why Me?"
I'll never entertain that impulse again—you have
shown me how futile that attitude is.

My first notice of you was in 1948—your work at the
National Convention.  Our paths were to cross many times
after that.  I chased you around Wisconsin during the
Humphrey-Kennedy primary.  I clapped and yelled with
you when Adlai Stevenson was nominated in Los Angeles in
1960.  I rejoiced in your Vice-Presidency, anguished with
you over Vietnam, agreed with you, disagreed with you—
but never stopped admiring the resolute way you formed
your opinions.

You, sir, are more than a Senator or public servant.
You are that precious American commodity we call a
Statesman.

You are a true Guiding Light—and you will shine forever.

Sincerely,

Dick Chapman

HUBERT H. HUMPHREY
MINNESOTA

## United States Senate
WASHINGTON, D.C. 20510

November 7, 1977

Mr. Dick Chapman
WCCO Radio
625 Second Avenue South
Minneapolis, Minnesota  55402

Dear Dick:

You have warmed my heart and lifted my spirits
with your letter of October 26.  Thanks so much
for all you had to say.  I hadn't known about
your disability and the attack of Multiple Sclerosis.
Indeed these troubles are enough to cause anyone to
despair.  But you and I both know that every day that
the good Lord gives us we must make the most of.  A
strong faith and good spirit is the best medicine there
is.

Some time ago, I heard a minister say that it isn't
what you have lost, it's what you have left.  That's
the way I feel.  I know I am not as strong as I once
was.  I can't do as much.  But I have enough left to
make life worthwhile and you have proved one thousand
times over that despite problems, you are a man of
great spirit.  God bless you and let's stay in touch.

Sincerely,

Hubert H.

Hubert H. Humphrey

I was pressed into service at Twin Cities International when Air Force One arrived. On such a sad occasion I was doing fine until a spectator, a middle-aged Black man, walked past me with heavy tears in his eyes. From that point on, the two days of coverage was a struggle to keep from breaking down myself.

I was assigned to the cemetery itself the following day. There I had to struggle not only with my emotions, but with bitter cold. Security arrangements closed the cemetery gates at 1:30 p.m. I was called upon to provide several live reports from 1:30 to 5:15 when the burial ceremony commenced. I'm sure I would have suffered frostbitten feet or hands had I not been able to catch brief warm-ups in the squad cars of obliging police officers. Other reporters suffered too. On one occasion, a young female camera operator from Minnesota Public Television climbed down from an icy, windswept camera platform for a warm-up. She told the officers her feet had been hurting in the cold for hours but the pain had gone away about 20 minutes ago. That's a sure sign of frostbite. She didn't know that. The officers did. They whisked her to a nearby ambulance.

Timing on the day was non-existent. The schedule was running extremely late. What do you talk about from a frozen cemetery for four hours. I drug up Hubert stories from the past out of my memory, trying to keep the tears from my voice. I described the solemn surroundings. I fought the cold.

Suddenly, during a live report, I glanced skyward to see a flight of mallard ducks winging right across Hubert Humphrey's gravesite. They flew straight toward the setting sun. I was astounded. It was 10 below zero. What were they doing there?

The ducks were there for Hubert. They were Hubert's ducks. I said so on the air.

I'm glad I did because I touched some hearts. My mail showed it. Some sample letters are on the following pages.

For my sad work that day, I was awarded the Minnesota Page One Award from the Newspaper Guild and the Society of Professional Journalists-SDX. After the sadness passed, I felt honored to have helped people say goodby to Hubert.

Vice President Walter Mondale perhaps said it best when he said, "He taught us how to live—and in the end, he taught us how to die."

Jan.16, 1978

Gen. Manager
WCCO
625 2nd Ave. S.
Mpls. Mn. 55402

Dear Sirs,

What a reporter you have in Dick
Chapman! And what a contrast to hear
him do such a solemn job on such a sad
occasion as Senator Humphrey's burial.

We listen to him daily with his
regular news broadcasts, so often filled
with violence and world ailments. You
tend to forget that news broadcasters
have hearts and souls too.

After hearing Dick from the cemetery,
I'll never make that mistake again.


Truly,

*Ingrid Olsen*

Mrs. Ingrid Olsen
Minnetonka, Minn.

## The Minnesota State Automobile Association

7 TRAVELERS TRAIL, BURNSVILLE, MINNESOTA 55337 • PHONE 890-2500

Jan. 17, 1978

Dear Dick,

Last night I left the office at 5:00 PM, got in
the car, dialed up CCO and headed for home. When I
heard the beginning of your remote from Lakewood, my
first reaction was one of disappointment...disappointment
that I wouldn't be able to see the thing on TV. I
have a drive of over thirty minutes from my new job
here in Burnsville, so I quickly resigned myself to
getting the whole thing via radio.

And what a lucky move it was! Your play-by-play
(if you'll pardon the rather crude expression) was
beautiful, Dick. Just beautiful. Somehow watching
the proceedings through your description was much more
real to me than were the several episodes surrounding
Hubert's death that I <u>had</u> been able to catch on the
tube over the weekend. ...dressed against the January
cold...the lines winding to the gravesite from the
buses...the trees...the just-departed sunset...the
honor guard "snapping" to attention...the flock of
ducks winging directly overhead...the precise folding
of the flag and subsequent presentation to Muriel...and
so on.

I know that yours was not an easy assignment. But
you did a helluva job with it. You're very good at
what you do. Thankyou for doing it for me.

I hope and presume that all is well with you. Say
hi to Barbara for me.

Cordially,

John De Haven
Minnesota State Auto. Assn.

Jan. 17, 1978

WCCO Radio
WCCO Bldg.
Minneapolis, Minn.

Dear Sirs,

I write to suggest that a recording of Dick Chapman's
graveside report during Senator Humphrey's funeral
be preserved and set aside for the Humphrey family.

I'm sure Muriel, and the children, and grandsons and
granddaughters would treasure it at a later date when
sadness has disappeared. None of them could have seen
the whole touching picture as it was described by
Mr. Chapman. Nor would hhey have been aware of the
overflight Hubert's ducks, just before the ceremony.
Our home is nearby. I saw them too, but only after
Mr. Chapman spotted them. Had he not, I never would
have looked up.

Dick was right, God Bless him! They _were_ Hubert's ducks--
and yes, the Senator could see them.

You have a marvelous station. Dick Chapman's broadcast
is a prime example that should be preserved.

Sincerely,

Harold Stensrud
3540 Freemont Ave. S.
Mpls., Mn.

**SENATOR HUBERT HUMPHREY**

Shortly before his death, **Senator Hubert Humphrey** agreed to be "roasted" by the Minnesota Press Club to raise funds for journalism scholarships. **Dick Chapman**, who chaired and co-emceed, shared a joke with Hubert.

# 1965—BLIZZARDS, FLOODS, TORNADOES

It would be folly to try to enumerate the hundreds of big stories I covered during 36 years at WCCO Radio. But Winter and Spring of 1965 cannot be ignored.

It was a winter from Hell capped by the St. Patrick's Day blizzard. That storm closed every school in Minnesota for the first time in history. Virtually every highway was impassable. Trains were stranded for days in huge snowdrifts.

Thanks to the remaining snowcover and seasonal rains, Spring flooding was disastrous. Seventeen major watersheds, including the Minnesota, the St. Croix, the Mississippi rivers all went wild. WCCO Radio's Flood Service Center operated around the clock for 16 consecutive days.

One event marked the only time in my life I talked myself out of a speeding ticket.

Some barges broke loose on the flooded Minnesota and started drifting downstream toward the construction project that would become the new Cedar Avenue Bridge. The workers possibly might be unaware. It was a crisis.

Technical Engineer Chuck Kunze and I grabbed a portable transmitter and leapt into my car to rendezvous with a rented helicopter on the parking lot of the old Metropolitan stadium. I know I was doing 60 miles per hour when I ran into a radar trap on Cedar Avenue.

I must have been eloquent. I know I was talking at 100 miles per hour.

"Officer, it's an impending disaster! Loose barges! Guys hanging on the bridge! Our helicopter's waiting! We may be able to save lives!"

The cop put away his ticket book, but admonished us not to speed.

Looking back, I should have pressed my luck and asked him to escort us with red lights and sirens.

The story was a partial bust. They managed to corral the run-away barges before they got too far downstream.

I'll never forget that helicopter. It was an old Bell chopper fitted for crop-dusting. It was the only one I could find for rent. Media types from all over had gobbled up everything available as the flood story grew.

The first day we used it, we discovered the old crate had no power for our transmitter. It had a battery, but no charging system. The pilot used his battery only to start the thing, putting it on a charger in the hangar every night.

Kunze simply removed the battery from our own vehicle and tied it behind the cabin in the superstructure that goes back to the tail rotor. He tied it there with a rope!

The pilot remarked, "Well, the FAA will raise Hell if we crash!"

We also had no communication with ground control. We had to avoid the air traffic patterns around Twin Cities International Airport.

In order to hover over a flood crisis situation at St. Paul's Ford Plant, the pilot dropped off radar into the Minnesota River valley and flew low around Fort Snelling where the Minnesota joins the Mississippi. We stayed low in the valley to cover another problem spot at Hastings, and then I opted to fly up to Stillwater where the swollen St. Croix was pushing ice against the bottom of the bridge.

It was an extremely windy day—gusts to 40 and 45 mph out of the Northwest.

When I said Stillwater, the pilot said, "Are you nuts? We can walk there faster than fly against this wind." I told you it was an old crate.

Solution: drop down on the deck again and fly up the St. Croix

Valley below the bluffs and out of the wind. What a hairy ride—six feet off the St. Croix ice, and beneath a number of power lines. I'm sure that's illegal.

It paid off though. We could broadcast the sounds of dynamite being used to break up the ice that was threatening the bridge. And we ran into a bonus flying back downstream.

Here were a man and his family sandbagging around his walk-out patio. It was a neat home at river's edge. The guy had a six-foot sandbag barrier holding back the ice and water as the St. Croix pushed relentlessly downstream. He was a 'CCO fan and had been listening to our chopper reports. He picked up a phone, waved it at us, and called the station. Super! I could conduct a live interview with him from the hovering chopper. I'm live from our transmitter, he's live from his phone. Great stuff, as the wife and kids helped lug sandbags—I talked to them all. It was a valiant family that ultimately won the battle against the St. Croix.

Then came the fateful night of May 6, 1965.

A megastorm developed and spawned nine huge tornado funnels that touched down in 23 locations. Fourteen people died, 450 were injured and property damage topped $51 million.

It was a night no one can forget, least of all me. I happened to be on the air when the first funnel was sighted near Norwood-Young America just west of the Twin Cities. WCCO Radio was well prepared for weather warnings, but no one could have anticipated what was going to happen in the next few hours.

Meteorologist Joe Strube, in charge of the U.S. Weather Service at Twin Cities International, would later classify it as one of the largest megastorms on record. Funnel after funnel boiled down. Sometimes there were two on the ground at the same time. Just as we've learned that lightning *does* strike twice in the same spot, we learned that funnels can rake an area already devastated by an earlier touchdown.

And all these funnels were of major proportions. Strube told me later that the energy of the overall storm was so great that it ground up all the missing trees and houses into matter as small as woodchips or sawdust, and deposited it somewhere in Lake Superior.

As the insane night progressed, it was difficult to grasp the magnitude of the storm. It was difficult to believe that we were tracking one funnel here, another over there, even a third one somewhere else.

How could it be? It was as though the overall storm was like a gigantic beehive stinging the earth at will.

WCCO staffers dropped everything and rushed to work. I moved from a small studio to a large one where we had a bank of telephones especially installed for our massive coverage of the earlier flood story.

Thank God we still had them installed. Those phones played a major part in saving hundreds of lives.

Thank God for the quality of WCCO Radio listeners. They became our eyes. They became our funnel spotters.

At various times, I could put listeners on the air live from different locations and have them triangulate the twisters locations. First, Navarre, Excelsior and Spring Park around Lake Minnetonka. Later, North Minneapolis, Brooklyn Park, Brooklyn Center, Golden Valley and, finally, Fridley (probably the hardest hit of all). The listeners were magnificent. Not only could they pinpoint a funnel location, but they also could describe which way it was moving. We could warn people in the path—and you better believe we did. I can remember at least two listeners providing this vital service until the last minute when the funnel's proximity forced them into their basements.

I have a letter from a Fridley man who said he had hurried his family into a crawl space beneath his trailer home and listened to his transistor radio as his house was demolished. He wrote, "I can't tell you how weird it is to listen to the play-by-play of your own home's destruction."

We had one man on the air who said he was driving a small car in the Black Lake area of Lake Minnetonka. He became mesmerized by a funnel and stopped to watch, not realizing that another funnel was right behind him. That twister sucked up his car and deposited it into Black Lake. The man gave a graphic description of huddling on the floorboards as the little car twisted through the air. He said he lost track of everything until coming to his senses standing on shore and watching his headlights go out in 15 feet of water. Then he said, "I don't know how I got out! I don't know how I got to shore! I can't swim!"

One listener's report still tugs at my heart. He was a press operator for the Minnepolis StarTribune. Hearing the storm reports, he knew his paper would need all the staff they had. His pickup was smacked by a funnel in Brooklyn Center but he escaped with only small cuts, even though the winds shattered all the glass in his vehicle. He gave another graphic description of huddling on the truck's floor as glass rained in atop him.

This is the sad part. He was calling from a pay phone near a Junior High School. The building's roof and part of the upper floor were gone. This man was courageous and thoughtful enough to call to report that all the kids at a Boy Scout meeting were safe and uninjured in the school's basement. He just wanted the parents to know. As far ar I know, those comforting words were the last he ever spoke. We learned later that his truck was hit by another funnel, and he became one of those killed on that fateful night.

**THE FATEFUL NIGHT OF MAY 6, 1965**

'CCO's Flood Service Center became the center for tornado coverage that night. The reporters were (left to right) **Dick Chapman, Rob Brown, Bob Tibbitts** and **Charlie Boone**.

SUBURBAN LIFE
Sunday, May 9, 1965

## With Morningsider on 'CCO
# Edina's Dick Chapman Was 'Man of the Hour'

by Barry Warren

An Edina man who sat before a microphone in a downtown Minneapolis radio station and ad libbed for six-hours on a tornado disaster will remember that story with mixed emotions.

Dick Chapman, an announcer for WCCO-radio was in the studio when the first warnings of a 25-mile-an-hour tornado crossing Highway 7 in Minnetonka was given at 6:30 p.m., Thursday.

Not far from the funnel's path was his house at 4619 Casco Ave., Edina.

The funnel began to move northeast, toward Crystal, Fridley and Spring Lake Park. Chapman's coordinating efforts with two dozen staffers in the field became relatively routine - as disaster stories go - until new complications set in.

### Close to Home

A field man sighted another black whirling cloud forming over the Southdale shopping center at 66th St., and France Avd. S., It was about two miles from where his wife, Jean, and their four children, Connie, 10, Candi, 8, Tim, 6, and Mike, 5, were located at home.

With Chapman as anchor man in the studio was Charlie Boone, who lives in Morningside. The black cloud increased in its intensity over the Edina area. While the two men apprehensively sweated out that danger they maintained constant touch with what soon developed into a full-scale smashing disaster in other suburban areas.

The time went fast and slow. As Chapman hurried through the fact lists of death and distruction from both staff men and private citizens who pinpointed funnels throughout the area, he and his colleague worried over their own families' doom.

"You can't imagine how it feels to be reporting a disaster story when it is rapidly developing in your own home territory," Chapman said Friday, still shuffling through more reports from the studio's newsroom.

### "Creepy" Feeling

Describing the feeling as "creepy" while sitting in the broadcasting booth fingering files that in any moment could be duplicates of a personal tragedy, Chapman said it "was difficult to keep things straight."

Although the Southdale sighting became one of many sightings of tornados which never touched down in the Twin City area, Chapman's vigilence was perhaps keener as the night wore on into the early morning hours.

"My family went into the basement," Chapman added, "and like many families who can attribute their lives to the broadcasting, I give the most credit to all those people who kept in close contact with us while pinpointing the funnels.

### No "Kooks"

"We were fortunate in not getting any kooks on the line," he said. "There wasn't any wrong information during the period." Chapman referred to the sighters in the Glen Lake area who stood by throughout the full tornado impact.

A native of Kansas, Chapman reported a tornado out of Kansas City, Mo., for a radio-television station in 1956. Another time, as a young boy, he was in a tornado while visiting relatives on a farm in Oklahoma.

"They had a good old-fashioned storm cellar," he said.

But, the tornado in the Spring of 1965 will be the one to be remembered for Chapman. "It's difficult to control emotions when something like that is so close to home, and still be responsible to your listeners."

Sometimes a newsman wonders whether the business he is in is worth it all, but Chapman figures it was worth it Thursday, "when I was part of a team that succeeded in keeping a lot of people alive."

Lyon County Independent

WEDNESDAY, MAY 12, 1965

Whats Cookin'
BY COOK

### THE GOOD NEIGHBOR—
### MORE THAN A SLOGAN

WCCO Radio in Minneapolis and St. Paul uses a catch slogan that proclaims the station as "Good Neighbor to the Northwest."

Last Thursday night it proved, as it has on a number of occasions in the past, that its slogan is not just fancy words.

When funnel clouds and actual tornadoes appeared to be spawning out of a massive weather front like evil monsters, WCCO plunged into the thick of it.

I have heard a few emergency broadcasts here and there—a hurricane, a couple of flash floods, a blizzard – but I have never heard anything to even approach the job done by WCCO last Thursday night.

I feel that two staff members – Dick Chapman and Charles Boone – must be named for a great share of the accolades. Chapman and Boone were in it from the very first warning from the weather bureau. That was a little after 6:30 p.m. They stayed with it most of the night, although I deserted them around midnight.

When it became apparent that the storm was no run-of-the-mill hard blow, Chapman and Boone were quickly joined by other staff members, notably Chuck Lilligren and John Walker. One of the classic broadcasts was by Walker who was caught in a twister out in the Minnetonka area while checking on an earlier report. He took refuge under a knee hole desk with a metal top, as the storm passed directly overhead.

The striking thing about the broadcasts, to me, were the dramatic eye-witness accounts from people who were actually watching funnel clouds move across the area. Several such reporters were almost too excited to talk, but talk they did! One I recall especially could not see out the window and reach the telephone at the same time. He had someone looking out the window and yelling information to him, while he in turn relayed it to the radio by telephone.

I have no way of knowing how many lives were saved by Chapman and Boone as they tracked twisters and warned people in the paths of the storms to take shelter.

I'm pretty sure nobody else has any way of knowing, either. But I'll tell you this: If anybody wants to set up some kind of movement to present Chapman and Boone some small token of appreciation and regard, say like each an engraved wristwatch or something like that, count me in. And I wasn't near the tornado area.

Until something better comes along, I'll nominate the job done by Chapman and Boone as the finest public service by radio in a whole lot of years.

THE MINNEAPOLIS STAR     Thurs., May 13, 1965

## MANY PRAISE RADIO

Tornado survivors credited air raid sirens and radio news bulletins for warning them of danger last Thursday, and their grateful comments poured in to state Civil Defense headquarters today.

The weather bureau sounded about a score of Civil Defense sirens scattered around the Twin Cities area, the first time they had been used for anything except tests.

Some communities, including heavily. damaged Mound, Fridley and Spring Lake Park, do not have sirens, according to Robert Lewis, a Civil Defense spokesman in St. Paul.

Lewis said it is up to local governments to install the sirens.

"The sirens did the job quickly, efficiently, and simply," wrote one St. Paul doctor.

"There was little doubt in peoples minds on hearing the sirens that something of major import was about and, on turning on the radio, ample warning was provided."

He summed up the scores of letters and cards which were the first of thousands expected in response to Civil Defense chief Roy V. Aune's appeal for constructive, after-the-disaster comments on the disaster alert.

### Brief Confusion

Many of the letters told of momentary confusion about the meaning of the sirens, until people got further information from radio bulletins.

The letter writers were generous with their praise for radio.

"I can't say WCCO radio took the place of my husband in soothing my nerves, but it did give me proper instructions to follow," said a Wayzata woman who weathered the storm in her basement.

"WCCO did yeoman service," wrote a Mound man.

WCCO won the accolades of every writer who specified a radio station.

---

MINNEAPOLIS TRIBUNE

Fri., May 14, 1965

## Letters to Tribune

### Radio Warnings
### Appreciated

To the Editor: I join the many listeners who are so grateful to WCCO Radio. Their advice and warnings during the recent tornadoes saved many lives and kept people alert and well informed of the happenings in each area.

If any awards are to be made for being useful and helpful to the communities of Minnesota, WCCO Radio and its wonderful staff should head the list.
— **Mrs. J. .V. Kopueller, Edina.**

---

Brooklyn Center Press
**Wednesday, May 19, 1965**

\* \*      \* \*

## Radio Stations, Particularly WCCO, Did Outstanding Jobs During Recent Tornado

WE SALUTE THE radio personnel and media of this area, and WCCO in particular, for the finest funnel-by-funnel job of on-the-spot news reporting that probably resulted in saving thousands of lives in this area because of their active coverage. Listeners also kept the station alerted.

IN MANY INSTANCES, the funnel-by-funnel reports were made from near the points where the destructive forces were forming. The radio broadcasters took their lives into their hands when they ventured into some of the areas to give first hand reports of the storm to their stations. One of the broadcasters even took to the air to gather first hand information from that observation point. Little credit was given radio stations for their on-the-spot reporting during the flood.

EACH RADIO STATION lost a considerable amount of advertising revenue during the storm broadcasts because that was not the time to think of commercials. This donation of time was voluntary on the part of the stations in order to provide a service for their listeners.

BECAUSE plaques will probably never be given for the heroic work of the radio people, we suggest you write a letter to the particular station to which you were listening and express your thanks for being alive. Had it not been for the warnings of the radio stations you might have been included among the tornado victims.

THOUSANDS OF PEOPLE in this area will have a lot more respect for the radio media in the future because of the heroic and excellent work that was performed during the tornado. We express our thanks from a grateful public.

The New Brighton BULLETIN
Thursday, May 13, 1965

# New Brighton Commends WCCO

The New Brighton Village Council Tuesday night adopted the following resolution offered by Trustee Richard Andersen:

STATE OF MINNESOTA
COUNTY OF RAMSEY
VILLAGE OF NEW BRIGHTON

RESOLUTION COMMENDING AND EXPRESSING A VILLAGE THANKS TO WCCO RADIO AND ITS PERSONNEL FOR EXCEPTIONAL PUBLIC SERVICE

WHEREAS on Thursday evening, May 6, 1965 and Friday morning, May 7, 1965 a severe disaster in the form of tornadoes, wind, hail and rain struck the metropolitan areas of Minneapolis and St. Paul and parts of the State of Minnesota and Wisconsin and

WHEREAS the people of these areas were in grave danger and

WHEREAS notification of the storm's movement and the methods people could use to protect themselves had to be made continually on an emergency basis and

WHEREAS WCCO Radio undertook this responsibility and

WHEREAS WCCO Radio abandoned all of its routine commitments and programing to keep the public informed and

WHEREAS this public service by WCCO is an outstanding example of the important function that private industry can and does perform for the public good in time of need and

WHEREAS the employees of WCCO performed admirably over this long and tragic period; foresaking their own families and

WHEREAS the services provided by WCCO Radio and its employees resulted in saving untold numbers from death or injury

NOW THEREFORE BE IT RESOLVED that the Village Council of the Village of New Brighton commends WCCO Radio and expresses its heartfelt thanks and appreciation to WCCO Radio and all of its employees; those known so well and particularly those unknown who make the others well known.

Adopted this 11th day of May, 1965.

Donald Anderson, Mayor
Robert Schaefer, Village Manager

Evelyn Ingram, Village Clerk

Wed., May 19, 1965    THE MINNEAPOLIS STAR

TV-RADIO CHATTER

# Drawing the Line on Storm Warnings

By FORREST POWERS
Minneapolis Star Staff Writer

Discussion of radio and television's role in advising listeners of the danger of severe storms has been widespread since the Twin Cities area experienced its night of terror May 6.

Some persons say storm warnings are broadcast too frequently and that they serve only to create panic. Others complain that some stations fail to do enough to alert the public of possible damaging storms.

The practice of allowing untrained weather observers to phone in reports during storms has been criticized as well.

Where would you draw the line?

Unquestionably, it is the responsibility of all radio and television stations to keep listeners posted on the possibility of severe weather. Since not all of us are tuned in to the first announcement of a tornado forecast or an acutal alert, it is imperative that the information be repeated.

In responsible hands, such announcements constitute a vital public service. On the other side of the coin are the stations that allow their announcers to shriek out word of a possible storm with enthusiasm befitting high school cheer leaders.

I recall listening to one Twin Cities' station a few years ago after a tornado forecast had been issued. For hours, the announcer conducted a hysterical storm scare campaign between mentions of his own name.

Toward evening a black cloud rolled up from the west and the station switchboard began jumping with calls from frightened listeners. Attempting to stem the panic, Mr. Rah Rah changed his tune by pooh-poohing the possibility of a twister.

The storm fizzled out, thankfully, but I don't know what happened to the announcer who performed this disservice. I haven't listened to the station since.

On the evening of May 6 I was tuned to WCCO radio. What I heard frightened me then as well, but there was good reason for fear on that night. This was a tornado alert, not a forecast.

WCCO did a magnificent job in keeping listeners informed on the progress of the storm. Perhaps other stations did as well or better. I can't compare station storm coverage because I was in no mood to twiddle dials during the emergency.

Granted, there were a number of false alarms among the phoned-in reports of funnel sightings. Outweighing them, however, were the accurate reports that did pinpoint the location of the tornadoes and undoubtedly helped save the lives of many persons.

* * *

# ANOKA County UNION

### 100th Year of Publication

Volume 100     10c Per Copy     Anoka, Anoka County, Minn., Friday, May 14, 1965—24 Pages          Number 37

# Editorial

## It Could Have Been Much Worse

Last Thursday night's destruction from the tornadoes could have been much worse.

We know that many of those who were in the full paths of those tornadoes that ripped through Fridley, Blaine and Spring Lake Park Thursday evening have lost most of what they owned. But the result could have been worse.

When one considers the death toll now placed at four in the north suburbs and when one realizes that of the 350 trailers parked at Fridley Terrace plus those on other locations, about 250, were a complete loss, the death toll might have been far greater than it was.

Those who live in trailers, have no place to go in face of an oncoming tornado. Some heard of the warning over the radio and they left the area. But there were no basements to go to, no place to hide. And we can only marvel that with nearly 5,000 persons out of their homes because of the swirling winds, only about one-half of 1% were fatalities. This is almost a miracle!

But miracle, though it is, credit must be given where credit is due and that is to the warnings given by WCCO Radio—the giant of the middle west.

Had it not been for WCCO Radio and its warnings, we are certain the death total would have been 100 times what it was. Had it not been for WCCO Radio, Mercy Hospital would not have had the staff on hand when the patients began rolling in. Had it not been . . . well for a number of things.

And so we say to WCCO Radio, "Well done thou good and faithful servant. You saw a job to be done and you did it. You cancelled your revenue bringing programs to give a continued alert to a fearful and apprehensive public and the services given were far beyond the normal call of duty. Some others helped but it was WCCO Radio —right here in our back yard—who ran with the ball and scored."

It was through WCCO that a call went out

And though radio and television could not stop the damage, the vast number of people who were able to prepare for the oncoming winds owe their lives to a better than excellent warning system.

Add the Civil Defense sirens to the warnings given and you can only give credit where credit is due.

After the storm hit, we can only pay tribute to the policemen of Fridley, Spring Lake Park, Blaine, Columbia Heights, and Anoka and the men of the Anoka county sheriff's office, Hennepin and Ramsey county sheriff's office and to the volunteer civil defense workers for the tremendous job they have done.

Gov. Karl Rolvaag called to duty three units of the 47th Viking Division of the Minnesota National Guard to help prevent looting and pilfering. He did not hesitate to call them out; they were there in rapid time.

All in all, the volunteers and the paid agencies did an exemplary job. The men and women of the medical profession, the men who manned the ambulances and other vehicles which brought patients to the hospitals, those who volunteered their services to help, all were fine.

There was just one "sour" note in the entire picture. That was the ever-present sightseer—the guy who just couldn't stay off the highways—he was just too curious.

It was the sightseer who caused most of the trouble even an hour or less after the tornado struck. It was this same sightseer who just couldn't or wouldn't stay out of the area.

And it was this curious group that loaded their cars with neighbors or family and gave the volunteer officials more trouble than anything else.

And a word of thanks to the staff, doctors, nurses, aids and all those who helped at the hospitals where the injured were treated. The

I have no doubt the death toll would have been appalling were it not for those marvelous listeners who acted as my eyes in spotting funnels and detailing their movements.

Imagine what it's like to be broadcasting funnel locations when one is spotted blocks from your own home. Where's my wife? Where are my kids? You gulp, cross your fingers and plunge on.

Radio people, television people and print reporters traditionally act as rivals—sometime's bitter rivals. Such was not true that night or the following days. As proof, I offer the following newspaper clippings on the previous pages.

I have in my possession a piece of brown paper. It looks as if it was torn from a shopping bag. Written in crayon are the words, "DEAR WCCO, THANK YOU FOR SAVING OUR LIVES." It's signed by nine members of a Cub Scout Den who weathered the storm in a church basement.

WCCO Radio captured the broadcast industry's top three national awards for life-saving public sevice: The Sigma Delta Chi (Professional Journalism Society) Award, the Columbia University Alfred I. Dupont Award, and the prestigious George Foster Peabody Award. No station, before or after, has won all three in the same year.

Of course, I'm proud. But I value that brown paper-bag note more than any of my awards.

## SPORTS

My years at WCCO were blessed with many encounters with luminaries in the world of sports. I either covered or brushed elbows with super stars, managers, coaches, owners, broadcasters or bums in all major leagues of all sports.

I was privileged to meet Gopher legends like Bernie Bierman, John

Kundla, John Mariucci, and Dick Siebert. There was a beer-guzzling bull session with Kundla, Maroosh, and Siebert that left my sides aching with laughter. Siebert's wit matched his baseball coaching prowess. Mariucci's insistence that any sport (save hockey) was wimpy, never wavered. Kundla had tales of his Gopher and Minneapolis Laker basketball squads you'd hardly believe.

I've had the pleasure to know George Mikan, Vern Mikkleson, and Elgin Baylor. It was the Mikan-Mikkleson-Pollard Laker teams that put professional basketball on the map.

Elgin Baylor started faking the minute he stepped off the team bus. He never looked straight ahead. He didn't have to. He had eyes in the back of his head. I was present in the old Minneapolis Armory the night Baylor set a league record with 82 points. He hit baskets from outside, from inside. He drove the lane for buckets with three guys on his back. He could not miss.

The Lakers had a rookie that game—"Hot Rod" Hundley. He got into the game long enough to score a single field goal. "Hot Rod" was notoriously cocky. He strode into his favorite eastside St. Paul bar after that game and his friends said, "Hey, Hot Rod! How'd you do?"

Hundley boasted, "Terrific! Baylor and I got 84 points."

I saw Gopher football coach Murray Warmath go from goat of the year to Coach of the Year in one season. In 1960 (after blowing the Rose Bowl) people actually tossed garbage on his lawn.

I covered Warmath's return to the Rose Bowl in 1961, and groaned when UCLA's Kermit Alexander took the first hand-off of the game for a 63 yard burst to the Gopher 12 yard line. But Warmath's forte was defense. His Gophers held the Bruins to a field goal, and those were the only points they allowed in powering to an easy victory. Murray learned from the 1960 defeat. In '61 he took his team away from all the Hollywood distractions, ensconcing them in a monastery one week before the game.

I'm pleased to have been able to fish with Warmath—an avid angler.

I'm pleased to have fished with Viking Hall-of-Famer Bud Grant. But I'm more pleased to have dueled with him during news conferences. The Old Trapper was as sly as they come. He could duck a question with the best of them—having heard virtually every question in the books. But, strangely, Bud would not duck a question properly thought out and properly presented. Any question, not inane, he'd do his best to answer squarely. The trick was to come up with the right questions.

Incidentally, the one (of four) Superbowls the Vikings could and should have won was against the Pittsburg Steeler team of Terry Bradshaw, Lynn Swann, and Franco Harris.

It was the Steeler's "Mean Joe" Greene and L.C. Greenwood who made the difference. The Vikings let 28 points get away from them. First, the great receiver John Gilliam went high for a catch at the Steeler goal line only to get popped so hard that the ball bounced 12 yards up field into the hands of a Steeler. It was a great defensive play. There went a TD.

Then on three different occasions, Fran Tarkenton had Gilliam wide open for touchdowns, only to have the passes knocked down—once by Greenwood and twice by Greene. Tarkenton was very good at throwing between the upraised hands of charging defenders—but not those two, on that given day.

On one of those sure TD passes, "Mean Joe" Greene was almost ten yards downfield as Tarkenton pulled one of his classic scrambles out of the pocket. Gilliam was streaking on a post pattern—wide open. Tarkenton fired, but somehow Greene jumped so high that he could deflect the ball even from such a distance. I hardly believed what I saw.

At a post game interview, Greene showed what a gentleman he was. He has real class. When he entered the media room everyone shouted, "How do you feel?" The victorious Greene said, "I feel great! But I know how they feel!" I jumped in with, "Joe, how high can you jump?"

He smiled and answered, "High enough, I guess."

Pro football's best play-by-play announcer was CBS and WCCO veteran Ray Scott. When he did TV, he had the knack of letting the picture tell the story. He didn't clutter up his description with unnecessary babble. You always knew the down, yards to go, and football's position. But he knew the viewers had eyes, and he just helped them follow the action.

In the Green Bay Packers' great years, they often ran an end-around with their huge steam-roller tight end, Leon Hart. Whenever that play developed, Ray Scott would merely say, "Big Leon!"

When he switched to WCCO Radio, without a TV picture, he adjusted magnificently. But then he had the benefit of color-man Grady Alderman. I think Grady (ex-Viking Pro-Bowl lineman) could have matched John Madden as a color-man. Alderman elected to pursue a rewarding career in pro football's front offices.

Still, I'll never forget Ahmad Rashad's "Hail Mary" game-winning catch at the old Metropolitan Stadium, sending the Vikes to the playoffs.

I was just behind Alderman in the broadcast booth. The bulky Grady leaped from his chair with such force, he ripped his head-set and microphone right off his face. Both cluttered noisely to the floor and Grady couldn't find them for a frantic moment.

Ex-Viking Paul Flatley is not too shabby as a color-man. He settled down drastically after a roisterous pro career. He wasn't fast, by wide receiver standards, but he had the moves and he had the hands. He was good enough to be a Viking Pro Bowler. He loved his beer.

Late in his Viking career, he was relegated to a back-up receiver. He arrived in the locker room one game day not only hung-over, but still slightly tipsy. QB Fran Tarkenton and Center Mick Tinglehoff smelled his breath and quickly muscled him to a far corner, lest Coach Norm Van Brocklin catch a whiff. The fines would have been costly. "Flats" didn't expect to play that day.

Would you believe, the starters got injured early, and Flatley (whatever condition) was pressed into service. He caught umpteen balls and scored three TD's for one of the best performances of his career. Never mind that he up-chucked after one well-executed tackle.

Baseball announcer Herb Carneal is one of a kind. Rightly, he's been honored with the Ford Frick Award as one of the best—an honor bestowed in 1996 at Cooperstown's Baseball Hall of Fame.

His forte is his knowledge of the game, his keen eye, his ability to deliver the action like a machine gun, and his no-nonsense approach.

He has a quick sense of humor that he prefers to keep under wraps. Only Halsey Hall and Frank Quilici could get him going. Halsey could break up anyone without even trying. But it was Quilici who spotted Carneal's droll wit and spent much of his time bringing it out of Carneal. Quilici was better at that than he was at playing shortstop or managing the Twins.

Carneal endured the tough years when the Twins were terrible. I could hear his tedium as the Twins bumbled through loss after loss. I even worried that Herb was falling down on the job. He must have felt it too, because he picked himself up and got it going, no matter how poorly the season went. It paid off. The Twins improved as Herb improved.

Herb Carneal was superb during the playoffs and the World Series of 1987 and 1991. He's never let down since.

Publicity photo for **DICK CHAPMAN'S** WCCO Ice Fishing Contest.
The Walleyes were purchased at Witt's Fish Market on Hennepin Ave.
Some newsroom wag posted the picture with the caption:
NAMATUCK—OUR NEW LEADER!

# THE CRAZY STUFF

Then there's all the crazy stuff you remember over 36 years at a 50,000 Watt Class 1-A Clear Channel giant.

Like bloopers!

Network legend Lowell Thomas already was famous for a hilarious break-up he suffered during a broadcast from Hershey, Pennslyvania. He was describing the town as the home of Hershey Chocolate Bars, and "Hersheys with nuts." Somehow that tickled him, and his infectious laughter kept creeping into his narrative despite all Lowell could do to control it. Lowell Thomas's laugh was in the same league as Cedric Adams'.

At any rate, Thomas was doing an oddity story about a 700 pound man. He finished with, "Last Tuesday the man suffered a fatal fart attack!" The blooper not only annihilated Lowell, but every announcer nationwide unlucky enough to follow him.

TV Sportscaster Hal Scott was video-taping an interview with the trainer for the Minnesota Vikings, attempting to learn if any players might be on drugs. The trainer absolutely denied this in his opening statement when Scott was informed that the sound was not right.

Hal interrupted the trainer with, "We gotta do this over again because you held the Goddam mike too close!" Wouldn't you know, the videotape was incorrectly cued and the whole sacrilegious episode was broadcast on Channel 4.

Complaints jammed not only Channel 4's switchboard but the one at WCCO Radio. There was such an overflow that complaints were diverted automatically to newsroom phones. I fielded many of them—all outraged viewers—except one. This guy said, "Ya know I've been watching television all day. That's the funniest thing I've seen. Could you re-run it?"

I'm not lily-white when it comes to bloopers myself.

I broke up one night while performing the unenviable task of doing a commercial for "Hollywood V-ette Brassieres" while my engineer's girl friend was visiting on the other side of the studio glass. As I labored to describe the uplifting support of said garment, he simply grabbed his sweater and stretched it straight ahead of his body.

That was at the same Missouri station where I boldly announced, "Stop out to Texaco Town and try some of their crisp, golden fried children!"

At WCCO, I once cited a day in medieval history when Martin Luther King Jr. nailed his theses to the door of the Catholic Cathedral hosting the Diet of Worms, Germany. (It was Martin Luther, Idiot!)

Twins baseball broadcasts often presented a problem if the game was delayed by rain. We'd be twiddling our thumbs, expecting to scratch the 10 p.m. News, when the skies would open up and the play-by-play crew would return things to the main studio. Often that meant we had done little to prepare for the newscast. And that surely meant "rip and read" raw copy from the wire service machines. Barbara Beerhalter, later to accept my proposal of marriage, was doing the ripping on one of those occasions. We were so pressed for time, no one could review anything. And little did we know a wire service writer was having a little fun for himself.

I'm reading raw copy about military action in Vietnam. I started getting tickled about an Allied assault on "The Black Virgin," a mountain held by the enemy. The wording kept getting trickier, and I completely lost it when the copy said, "by nightfall our troops had successfully penetrated 'The Black Virgin'."

But the classic was on the old 10 p.m. News when my sponsor was Beebee Hilltop Laboratories, manufacturers of feeds and medicines for various farm livestock.

For the first line of a commercial I said, "Little pigs have tiny orgasms!" (ORGANISMS—the word's supposed to be—ORGANISMS!)

I knew my mistake instantly. But I thought, keep going! Don't break up! Maybe nobody caught it! I managed to maintain control even though my engineer was doubled over in laughter. I was quite proud of my composure. I finished the whole newscast without breaking up.

Then I opened the broadcast booth sound door and there stood our switchboard operator. She was obviously flustered—so much so that her head-set still clung to her ears and the switchboard plug dangled across her breast.

She bellowed, "What in the world did you say?"

Only then did I break up.

## GULLIBLE'S TRAVELS

WCCO Radio's Sports Director for a few years was Paul Giel, the Gopher All-American who later became the University's Athletic Diector. Paul is a warm and likeable guy—but a bit gullible.

I always included him on our Fishing Opener broadcasts. In fact, we cooked up a routine during the live countdowns to midnight when Giel would throw out the first cast. It was nifty. As the seconds wound down, I'd say in hushed tones, "Paul is testing the wind. He's examined his reel drag. He's about ready to throw out the first official cast." After that anything might happen—unbeknownst to Paul.

On one occasion I told Paul, "When I point the mike at you I want you to yell, 'DIRTY ROTTEN RACKAFRATZ!'" He repeated it several times to get it right, "DIRTY ROTTEN RACKAFRATZ!"

When it came to the live broadcast, I went through the hushed, tense buildup counting down to midnight. A colleague stood nearby with a concealed fishing reel. Here's how it sounded on air: "Three, two, one— Midnight! Here's Paul Giel's first official cast!"

Whereupon I swung the mike to my colleague who yanked the line against the reel's drag, producing the unmistakable sound of a backlash. Fortunately, Paul had been sipping a few beers and was not paying close attention to the lead in. I shoved the mike in his face and he obliged with "DIRTY ROTTEN RACKAFRATZ!"

Listeners began to look forward to our midnight fishing countdowns. What would Giel do next? Paul became aware of his starring parts.

One opener, Paul kept badgering me as to what we were going to do for the famous midnight countdown. I put him off. I said, "We'll get to it when the time comes. Just play it by ear."

This time we were set up with a live mike on a dock right at water's edge. On the air, I continually expressed concern that Paul Giel had not arrived to throw out his official first cast. As midnight approached I said, "Oh! Here comes Paul! Hurry Paul! It's almost midnight!"

Whereupon another colleague galloped down the dock, noisily tramping the wooden boards so his running steps could be heard on the live mike. He swished right by Giel and flung a large rock into the lake—also clearly heard on mike. Giel was so dumbfounded he couldn't appreciate my description of efforts to rescue Paul from the water. I think that's the gag when Paul actually threatened me with fisticuffs.

'CCO Producer Jack Douglas was often a conspirator in these plots.

On one fishing opener, a group of Northwest Airline pilots staying at a nearby resort sent the 'CCO crew a case of champagne. I have a good idea where they got it. Jack Douglas dreamed up the idea of taking a champagne sauna at our resort's facilities.

They had a nice pool and adjoining sauna with a neat sign that said "Closed!"

P. R. Director Rob Brown, Giel and I thought highly of Douglas's idea. Jack had stashed most of the bubbly in a landing net tucked beneath a dock in the chilly lake. He retrieved it after a slight detour. Actually it was a slight misstep that landed him in the water. We had no swimming suits, but the pool lights were off anyway. So we crept nakedly into the sauna, sipped champagne, and doused the hot sauna coals with the same bubbly.

Well, when you get so hot in a sauna, you've got to cool off in the pool. So we skinny-dipped. It may have been the effect of the champagne (both sipped and inhaled off the sauna coals) that caused someone to dream up a diving contest.

Man, I tell you we were doing back flips, gainers, full-twisting one-and-a-halfs—completely in the buff. We were having a ball.

It wasn't until the next day that we discovered we had an audience for the entire performance. Two young couples from White Bear Lake had dropped by to see the 'CCO Crew and took the wrong path to the main lodge. It led right by the pool. Thankfully, they didn't have cameras.

Chubby 'CCO Engineer Jimmy Erickson was the assigned engineer when Paul Giel, Rob Brown and I broadcast the first Winnipeg to St. Paul 500 Snowmobile Race.

What a chore! Sub-zero mornings when the racers took off. Harrowing rides in the 'CCO van along icy roads trying to reach the day's finish line before the contestants did. And we were doing live reports scattered through the day.

The night before the race we met the president of Canada's O'Keefe's Brewery. The gentleman gave us a double case of O'Keefe's fine beer. You may not believe it, but our schedule was so hectic that we didn't gulp right through it. Early to rise—late to bed—we collapsed each night in a different motel, seldom taking showers or climbing out of our snowmobile suits.

Finally, on the eve of the last race day we found ourselves in St. Cloud at the good old Saint Germaine Hotel. And for the first time we had some time to spare. Hot showers around—clean skivvies and socks. Hey, let's order up some room service sandwiches.

AND HEY, aren't there a few O'Keefe's left down in the van.

Jim Erickson allowed as though there were at least five, maybe six. Erickson was appointed to retrieve them.

Well, the Saint Germaine was a swank joint compared to our previous lodgings. Furthermore, it featured a grand lobby Erickson had to traverse to retrieve the beers.

Jimmy didn't think it right to march through the crowded lobby brandishing a bunch of beers. And he didn't have a sack. So he gently slipped them down the pant legs of his snowmobile suit—three on one side, three on the other. Make that two on the other because the sixth and final beer went down too hard and broke.

Completely discumbobulated, he strode through the lobby with his boots foaming. Before he reached the elevator, a top exploded off a beer in the other pantleg and he left a trail of delicious O'Keefe's beer all the way to room 507. It was a delicate, but hilarious task, getting all the glass and suds out of Erickson's snowmobile boots.

Jimmy Erickson is the wag who learned that I had requested from management an electric typewriter. My bout with Multiple Sclerosis was affecting the strength and dexterity in my hands. When Erickson learned my request had been denied, he took a pencil and an extension cord and deftly crafted me an "electric pencil." It still adorns my wall.

Speaking of wags, there was Lou Latson, the first black performer hired by WCCO Radio. He was quite talented and particularly funny. His quick wit seemed to explode from nowhere.

Complaining about an inept engineer he remarked, "He's the only guy in the business who can wow "Capitol Cloakroom."

"Capitol Cloakroom" was a half-hour CBS political broadcast we recorded for later airing. It was recorded on disk. To "wow" a disk is to cue it improperly so it's off-speed when activated.

Latson always referred to St. Paul as Dodge City. He claimed he loved to go there and carouse with his (I'm sure mythical) friend, "Rush Out Red."

I joked with him once about taking up the sport of snowshoeing. He said, "Man, I'm waiting for the platform models."

As for snowmobiling, he said, "Not unless it's a closed air-conditioned cab with color TV."

When I tried to get him interested in fishing he said, "Man, you want me to go out there and put one little string down in all that water—no way!"

### LURES & LAUGHS

Frequently, those fishing openers were anything but tame.

At Lake Winnibigoshish one year, Governor Karl Rolvaag joined us and brought along the Department of Natural Resources Commissioner Ted Shields. In my opinion, he was one of Minnesota's best. Governor

Rolvaag's problems with alcohol were no secret, but he was normally careful while in office to do his drinking in relative private—not in public. Friday night before opening, he had a small party in his room which was situated directly above the resort swimming pool.

The pool had a neat arrow, pointing at the water, which proclaimed "Heated Pool."

Several of us, Ted Shields included, forayed into Bena and sipped a few beers in the well-known tavern built in the shape of a muskie. You walked in through the tooth-filled gaping mouth of our famed fighting fish.

Perhaps we sipped a few too many beers. Ted Shields deserted us. Others followed suit, leaving only myself and 'CCO salesman Wally Wilbur to return to our resort alone.

Well, you know how things go. We were enchanted by that little "Heated Pool."

We debated—no, we dared each other. A coin toss. I'd go first, but only if Wally followed immediately. Again, no swimming suits— undershorts would suffice.

It was a chilly mid-May night. No lights on the pool save those spilling from the party in Gov. Rolvaag's room.

Wally and I stripped, poised on the diving board, I took off and dove into the water.

It was as cold as a mountain stream! The sign lied! I surfaced and tried to wave Wally off. My agonizing scream told him instantly that there was a problem.

Too late! Wally was in mid-air behind me. Man, was it funny though to see the look on his face and watch him try to claw mid-air to keep from hitting that icy water. I'm positive we were out of there and dressed in perhaps five seconds.

The Governor? He merely remarked, "Ya know, I think some idiots took a swim last night."

A similar swimming pool event occurred at Island View Resort on Gull Lake. It was another 'CCO fishing opener with DNR Commissioner Ted Shields an invited guest again. This time his wife accompanied him, and we learned straight away that she was a pert, sharp, delightful lady.

Also in attendance was 'CCO Staffer Dick Stuck, an old fishing buddy of mine who later saw the light and became a successful P.R. and ad man in his own firm. Stuck was a notorious practical joker.

No one—absolutely no one—is exempt from practical jokes on fishing openers.

After working to provide fishing reports through the weekend, we found time for some relaxation at poolside about mid-afternoon on Sunday. The pool had a sign that read "Heated Pool." Sound familiar? No swimming suits again. Sound familiar?

I, in my wise brilliance, had already tested the water with my little fingers. It was colder than a mountain stream.

A couple of colleagues, 'CCO Controller Bill Fuhrman and aforementioned Engineer Jim Erickson, stripped to undershorts and took the plunge. Lots of screaming and yelling. Quickly, they climbed out.

Ah, but here came Dick Stuck. What an opportunity!

As he approached the pool area, I persuaded my colleagues to re-enter the pool and pretend the sign was correct and that they were all enjoying a relaxing dip.

Stuck bit! Well, he nibbled.

Fuhrman yelled, "Come on in. It's like a warm bath."

This was a magnificent piece of acting, considering Fuhrman's lips were turning blue.

Stuck complained he had no swimsuit.

Erickson coaxed him, "It's okay, we're both in our skivvies—besides there are no women around."

Stuck stripped to his boxer shorts, but still hesitated. He's not an easy mark, having played a few pranks of his own over the years. I swear he was about to test the water with his toe when Mrs. Ted Shields suddenly arrived.

Stuck was embarrassed and reached for his trousers. He took his eyes off me long enough for me to give Mrs. Shields a pleading look.

She got the scam immediately. She put her hand in the pool and said, "Why it's like a warm bath."

Stuck dropped his trousers and dove into the pool.

A stuck pig (pardon the pun) couldn't have screamed louder. Dick Stuck's body hit the pool surface as though a giant hand had skipped a rock.

Score one for the good guys.

Mrs. Shields was doubled with laughter. The rest of us were tripled. Bless her heart for being so sharp as to assess our scam so quickly and put the final spring in the trap.

As I've said, Dick Stuck has pulled a few fast ones of his own.

One came to pass on Reindeer Lake in far north Canada. Stuck, myself and two other guys decided to escape the comforts of the main lodge and camp our way into big lake trout territory.

We collared two guides, gathered tents, food, 70 gallons of extra gasoline, and one extra outboard motor. We stowed everything into two 16 foot boats, and spent a week roaming northward on 100 mile long Reindeer Lake. We'd fish and move—fish and move—each night setting up a new campsight.

Have I mentioned somewhere that I have a wooden leg?

There's a lot to be said for wooden legs. One foot never gets wet or cold. You've always got a spare change of socks—just switch one with the other.

But when building a campfire, wooden legs are the greatest things since duct tape and WD-40. Your wooden shin acts as a pefect fulcrum for breaking firewood. Just grasp the kindling firmly in two hands and crack it across the old wooden leg. It's the quickest, most efficient method ever devised.

Thats what I did all week long—crack firewood over my leg—for breakfast fires, shore lunch fires, evening cocktail-hour fires. My buddies just took it for granted. Pile all the firewood at Chapman's feet.

Ah, but our Indian guides were Crees. Crees are a marvelous bunch. They are proud, hardworking, honest, experienced in the wild—but they are quite reticent—very tight-lipped. They fear intruding on another man's space. Our two guides didn't even tell us they had become lost during our long foray up the lake. They'd never been there before. We had maps. We straightened them out and assured them it was nothing to be ashamed of. We were beginning to break through their reticence, we thought, but they remained strangely apart in a prolonged camp setting that normally knits a group together.

Our Cree guides did not know of my artificial leg. They just watched and said nothing as I cracked firewood all week long.

Roll ahead to our last day out. We had fished up the lake and back. We were out of beer and whiskey. Two 16 foot boats don't allow carrying much non-essentials.

We were virtually out of food. We'd eaten almost nothing but fish for most of the week (the T-bones went the first night.) We had gone through the extra outboard motor for parts to fix the other two. We were almost out of gasoline. Would you believe half-a-gallon between two boats? We were a motley crew, dirty and unshaven, as we returned to the main lodge island at almost midnight on a Friday. The sun is still up that late, that time of the year, that far north. But everyone in camp was abed.

To Hell with that! We were voyageurs! We pounded on doors and got the staff to rustle us up some steaks, whiskey and beer. We gorged ourselves. We overdrank. It was Bacchanalia.

The next morning, I was the last to get shaved, the last to walk to the main lodge for breakfast. As I ambled down the trail, I noticed Indians ahead of me would vacate the walkway and swish into the woods. There were a lot of Indians around. This was break day. New guests arriving. Old guests leaving. Guides day off, so all their wives and kids were in camp for the day.

As I neared the main lodge, I was sure the Indians, young and old, were avoiding me. Inside I said as much to my buddies, "It's weird. They just run into the bush. I took a good shower. I know it ain't that!"

Enter Dick Stuck who sought out one of the more sociable Cree guides and asked about Chapman's apparent blackball.

The guide said, "Breaks firewood over his leg!"

It was all over camp. The man's inhuman. The Cree were mystified.

Stuck decided to whip up one of his gags. He got a young Canadian staffer to pile up some firewood at our cabin. After breakfast he went about rounding up all the Indians in camp. There they were—men, women, children—must have been one hundred or so, set up in a semi-circle for the Dick Stuck sideshow on our cabin steps.

Stuck would hand me a piece of firewood and shout, "Five dollars to anyone who can do this!"

Whereupon I would crack the firewood in pieces across my leg. The Indians merely grunted.

Stuck would select a larger piece and yell, "Ten dollars for anyone who can do this!"

Same deal—crack—across the leg. Indians grunt again.

Stuck yelled, "Two pieces of firewood! Twenty dollars!"

Wham! I broke two pieces at once, and my wristwatch band to boot. Indians only grunt.

As a finale we stuck an ice-pick into my leg.

Later one Cree approached Dick Stuck and asked, "How he do that?"

Stuck said, "It's a trick. He really doesn't break the wood over his leg. Just before he hits his leg, he snaps it in his bare hands."

The guide merely grunted.

One year later we returned to the same camp. Stuck and I helped a young Cree guide load our boats. I had never seen the Indian before. Stuck pointed to me and said to him, "Do you know who this is?"

The guide grunted, nodded his head, and said, "That's Old Iron Leg!"

I had a pang of conscience for having deceived such innocent and naive people whom I had come to admire. I showed my wooden leg to everyone. I don't believe any of them had ever seen one. But they were delighted. Now we had a closer bond. And to this day, I'm known among that Cree band as "Old Iron Leg."

My old iron leg caught another guy off base. He was anything but innocent and naive like the Cree.

His name was Dan McGuire. We called him "Dangerous Dan McGrew." He ran a small bar and short order restaurant on the east fork of the Chippewa River near Hayward, Wisconsin. The river flows into the Chippewa Flowage—"The Chip" to many avid muskie anglers—home of world-record-sized muskies. Dangerous Dan was an avid angler and one of your better muskie experts.

He, too, was unaware of my wooden leg. I've had the darn thing so long I just forget about it.

On my first muskie outing with McGuire, I hooked a small muskie—barely legal size of maybe 12 to 15 pounds. He was a bit fiesty as I tried to release him and he thrashed around at my feet, neatly burying the treble hooks of my lure into my wooden leg. Anxious to release the fish before it hurt itself, I grabbed a pair of long-nose pliers and eased the hooks from the muskie's mouth. After slipping the fish back into the water, I yanked the lure out of my leg and continued casting. I think I said something cavalier like, "Maybe there's a bigger one around here."

McGuire grunted, very much as the Cree had grunted in my far north vaudeville show.

Much later that night after hamburgers and beers at McGuire's bar, I was playing bumper pool with a buddy. McGuire was tending bar. He couldn't stand it anymore.

He waved another buddy over and nodded at me with the remark, "There's the toughest son-of-a-bitch I've ever seen!"

"Why's that?" said my pal.

"Takes fishhooks out of his leg with a pair of pliers," said McGuire.

We never let McGuire forget it.

I've already detailed two skinny-dip stories. This one may make you think I'm some sort of nudist freak. I'm not.

However, I was fishing in Canada one summer while staying on "The Lord Rapala." That was Ray Ostrom's houseboat, named after the fishing lure that made him and his partner millionaires. It was tucked into a secluded cove—so secluded one never gave a second thought to wandering around unclothed.

The houseboat featured a generator that provided power on demand. It would sit idle unless a light was turned on, whereupon it started automatically.

One sunny morning, I climbed atop the houseboat to check the generator's oil. I happened to be stark naked.

No lights were on. The generator sat idle. The dip-stick showed some oil was needed. I uncapped the oil receptacle and prepared to add a quart.

I had forgotten one thing. The houseboat also featured an electric refrigerator-freezer.

At that moment, the refrigerator kicked in and so did the generator. It sprayed hot oil on me from nipples to kneecaps. I groped wildly for the master switch and managed to stop the generator, but not before it covered me and half the top deck with black sludgy oil.

I was about to yell below deck for some rags when I heard—of all things—an outboard motor.

For the first time in history, someone found our secluded cove. It was a man and wife fishing with a guide. My god! They came trolling right into the cove!

I sprawled on my belly to get out of sight. Wouldn't you know it? They took their time admiring the houseboat and flipping lures all over the place. All this while I'm spread-eagled in a pool of hot, sludgy oil on the roof.

It was so ridiculous I started laughing. I clamped my hand over my mouth for fear of being heard. All that accomplished was to spread the oil all over my face.

They heard me all right. But they couldn't see me. Maybe they thought I was a ghost. At any rate they finally went on their way, and it took three sudsy showers to get my body clean.

### "GOOD NEIGHBOR" TOURS

During my years at WCCO Radio, I was called upon to lead very few "WCCO Radio Good Neighbor Tours." But that's just fine, because the few I got were plums. You can have Hawaii—I'll take Russia or Africa!

### OUT OF AFRICA

I hosted a delightful group, flying first from Twin Cities International to Rome, then to Africa at Entebbe-Kampala in Uganda. Little did we know that small aiport was to be the scene later of the bloody firefight between Israeli Commandos and the high jackers of an El Al jetliner.

We saw Victoria Falls on the Zambezi, Murchison Falls on the Upper Nile and various wild game veldts of Uganda, Kenya, Tanzania, Dar Es Salaam, Zambia, Rhodesia (now Zimbabwe) and South Africa. Much of it was by road (and off road) in Volkswagen Cambi campers fitted with sliding roofs for photography. I cannot describe the camera opportunities. I shot miles of film on a Super-8 movie camera. This may help give you an idea. On the Upper Nile near Murchison Falls, I was filming crocodiles. I spotted a big one and zoomed in as he basked in the sun. Suddenly a huge one appeared from beneath some overhanging brush—sauntering into the river. So help me, it was twice as long as what I thought was the big one. Does 25 feet sound incredible? He seemed that long. I was unable to get an accurate measurement since I didn't want to get my feet wet.

Huge hippos lolled in the same waters. They're vegetarian, but are not averse to attacking anything that threatens their young. I got a great shot of a bull hippo charging our motorlaunch with that huge mouth agape.

At one lodge, someone had just landed a 99 pound Nile Perch. So help me they look exactly like a giant Largemouth Bass. I had my picture taken with it, and promptly lost the print. Rats!

Once we motored by a huge snake that established itself as a Cobra by lifting that head and flaring its hood. Our driver, an African native, had cranked up his window quickly and displayed the only fear I'd seen on the entire trip. He declined my request to return for a possible picture, explaining that the particular region was noted for several types of cobra, including some spitting cobras that are accurate up to 12 feet.

We photographed leopards at Secret Valley—a resort at the bamboo jungle foothills of Mount Kenya. It's the only place in the world to see leopards in their natural habitat. Leopards are nocturnal feeders, and the resort owners had spent years coaxing a nearby leopard family to become accustomed to artificial light at a feeding platform. The light was called "artificial moonlight" just enough for fast film. The resort was on stilts, some 40 feet high, bringing it to the level of the feeding platform near a watering hole.

I rode aside a co-owner of the resort, driving a British Lorry, down a narrow, muddy path (you wouldn't call it a road). He struggled with the slipperyness and said the Lorrys were a "bugger" to get back on the road if you slipped off. This guy was an ex-Sergeant Major in the British Army—a hulk of a man, right out of the movies. Between us was a high powered rifle. Upon arrival, some 100 feet from the lodge, he turned and said, "Ladies and Gentlemen, no talking please. I want complete silence until we're inside the lodge." Whereupon he thrust two huge cartridges into his rifle.

They looked like 50 caliber machine gun bullets to me. He explained later he feels noise is a big attrraction to jungle predators. Kenyan law requires tourists to be accompanied by a licensed big-game hunter in the wild. His insistence on silence, he thinks, is why he's never fired his weapon during that 100 foot trek. I obeyed him instantly because the first thing I saw as I stepped from the Lorry was a huge cat print in the mud. And looking up into the jungle, not two feet away, I couldn't see a foot into the heavy growth.

The routine was to arrive at dusk, enjoy dinner, and settle down to await the big cats' arrivals, usually after midnight. The incredible strength and grace of the first leopard was obvious when the cat, from a standing start, leapt to the top of that platform in two bounds. You could hardly hear the claws grasp the pole in mid-flight. Flashless cameras clicked. My movie camera rolled. Everyone was quiet until someone coughed, and the leopard was down and gone in a silent flash.

Our Sergeant Major calmly told the guests re-assembled inside, "That was a three-year-old female named Sheba. We think she's pregnant. We hope so because they sometimes bring their cubs with them." We saw several other leopards that night. No one went to bed.

Our Sergeant Major regaled us with stories. He repeated he'd never had to fire his weapon to protect guests. He echoed other big game hunters who say the most dangerous beast in the bush is the Cape Buffalo.

"They always see you before you can see them, and if they decide to charge, you've got bloody little time to get a shot off," he said.

Plus, he said, that shot has to be accurate. If you hit them in the thick bony nodule atop those wicked horns, it just makes them madder. The shot has to be placed behind the horns into the upper neck or spinal column, very much like a matador's sword thrust at a bullfight.

He told us of a close friend, forced to fire on a charging Cape, only to have his gun misfire. The buffalo ripped him from groin to mid-chest and hurled him 20 feet away.

The only thing that saved him was a huge abandoned ant-mound. African termites construct them 8 to 10 feet tall. The hunter managed to crawl into the excavated base of the mound and hide while the buffalo snorted around looking for another assault. Nearby villagers saved the man who surely would have bled to death had the buffalo not wandered away. Our Sergeant Major said his friend quit his big-game hunting career and returned to England.

He also told us of his co-owner partner, a native of India. On the grand opening attended by guests up to the level of royalty, something went amiss with the "artificial moonlight" generator—muffled and buried deep in the jungle. With twilight descending, he went afoot to fix it without his gun. As he returned on the skimpy path, the guests were horrified to spot a pair of adult leopards stalking him. None among them were hunters. One of the staff was smart enough to warn everyone not to shout warnings. The owner made it back—but the two cats had closed their stalking margin considerably before he did.

Many East Indians do not take alchohol as per their religion. This particular Indian, took his first drink that evening—about half a pint of Scotch in one gulp.

I can say this about Secret Valley. It's much more fascinating than the more advertised Treetops Lodge co-founded by movie star William Holden. We stopped there too, but only for lunch and a swim in their very nice pool. Their lodge also is built on stilts by a watering hole. But they have no leopards.

Our native guides were delights. They spoke many languages, including various tribal dialects. They nicknamed me Dik-Dik—after a miniature native antelope.

Once we drove off road to get pictures of an elephant family with youngsters. A young adult bull didn't like us much. He flared his big floppy ears, hoisted his trunk and tail, trumpeted and faked a charge. Each time the driver would gun our engine and move the van a few yards until the bull veered off.

"He's just bluffing," he said.

However, on about the fourth charge, he wasn't bluffing anymore!

That bull really came! You'd be amazed how fast they can accelerate. This time our driver accelerated too, and kept on accelerating out of there.

This same guide spotted a rare black rhinocerous. He eased up close, taking advantage of the fact rhinos are notoriously near-sighted. He kept downwind because rhinos smell and hear very well. This monster heaved himself up out of his mud hole and squinted at us with his nose sniffing and his ears twitching. He could hear us but couldn't see us or smell us. It made for great pictures until one of those dreaded Cape Buffalos stepped out from some nearby brush.

"No pictures!" hissed our driver. "Everyone be quiet and don't move."

The Cape could see us, hear us and smell us. We were trapped between two of the most powerful beasts in all of Africa. That buffalo ambled around, taking a few steps toward us, then lost interest and wandered back into the bush. The driver would have burned rubber getting out of there if we had been on pavement.

He later assured us that we were safe, explaining that both animals have been known to charge vehicles—even overturn them. But we would have been safe inside.

I asked, "Then why did you insist on silence and high-tail it out of there?"

He said, "The company doesn't like it if animals dent up the buses."

We were in one area where the guide didn't understand the dialect. I could tell he was uneasy as he warned us to refrain from photographing tribesmen or tribeswomen without permission. Some tribes think cameras capture and steal their souls.

As we were driving away, wouldn't you know it, one of our group took a picture anyway. The big Masai tribesman hurled his ever present spear at the vehicle and damn near hit us.

We met a fellow Minnesotan in Uganda who had been in that country several years as a U.S. agricultural adviser. He'd spent time with various tribes, one that lived in complete nakedness. It was here he learned an amazing story.

There is an incurable disease bred in some African waters called Belle Harte. It's carried by a parasite that buries itself beneath the skin and infects the bloodstream. It's insidious because the symptoms don't appear until months after being infected. It's fatal. Researchers have been struggling for decades to define it, or at least treat it. Our Minnesota friend told us of three researchers who died, insisting they had become immune.

Research has failed to make any strides against Belle Harte, but African natives have lived with the threat for centuries and beaten it by simple methods. Somehow they discovered what causes the disease and they take measures to be sure they're not infected by the parasite. Each time they bathe, they examine each other for tell-tale bites. If any are found, the parasites are dug out with crude bone needles.

Our Minnesotan said that presents a unique problem for this particular naked tribe. The standard of beauty for tribal maidens is the buttocks. He said he'd seen eligible suitors, seeking a bride, ask for and receive parental permission to examine and fondle the buttocks of available maidens. Sometimes a proud poppa would line his daughters up for the bachelor to march behind, examining and caressing each fanny.

The problem is the Belle Harte parasite. How would a fanny look if it was full of pock marks made by bone needles?

No problem.

Our Minnesota friend said the tribe is fastidious. Youngsters bathe in infected waters and go through the bone needle ritual only until the age of puberty. Thereafter, the young women avoid the infected waters and cleanse themselves with native oils and sand or soapstones. Voila!  A perfect posterier!

Travel certainly is broadening. Bad joke!

I won't soon forget the Ngorongoro Crater. It's the site of a huge meteorite crash that created one of the world's calderas—a fascinating natural game preserve. Perfectly round, it hosts a seasonal shallow lake filled in the wet season with zillions of pink flamingoes. It has a fissure, or opening, at one ridge as the only way in or out of the crater. That opening is a portal to and from Tanzania's adjoining Serengeti—teeming with wildlife of every kind. Curiously, lions, elands, gazelles, gnus, zebras, whatever— wander in and out of the crater in perfect proportion to the food chain. No species ever overpopulates or thins out. The animal balance remains virtually unchanged.

Tourists like us drive into the crater down a single perilous road in Landrovers. It's an all-day affair, shooting pictures 'til you drop. You can stop within feet of a pride of lions who pay very little attention to you. You must stay in the vehicle, however.

The day is highlighted by a lunch stop in a rustic wooden-walled compound with the old sharp-pointed timbers like in the King Kong movie. Once inside, the gate is closed for protection so you can stretch and enjoy sandwiches and Elephant Beer, a rather good local brew. I had two. That was a mistake!

As we're driving around past any number of lions that afternoon, nature called. It didn't call. It demanded! I asked the driver about the whereabouts of the nearest toilet. Yep! There aren't any. And, "You must stay in the vehicle, Sahib!"

There were four of us in back—one woman up front. It's not long before every passenger is aware of my painful condition and trying not to chuckle about it. I'm gritting my teeth. My eyes are crossed. Suddenly—a miracle—deliverance!

The biggest, ugliest, flying insect I've ever seen zips through the open window and slams into the bosom of the woman in the front seat. She's screaming bloody murder as that bug buzzes around sounding like a chain saw. The driver is trying to shoo the thing away. The other passengers are ducking.

Me?

I jumped out the back and did my business. I tell you if a lion had approached, I could have driven him off with the power of my rest stop. I was finished and back in the Landrover before the battle of the bug was over. No one had seen me. That bug attracted too much attention.

I believe it was 15 or 20 minutes before my friends noticed the relaxed look on my face. Only then did it sink in, and those rat-finks told the driver. He doubled up with laughter and joked that he'd have to turn me in to the preserve Rangers, who'd give me a ticket for violating the stay-in-the-vehicle rule.

I'd have paid it gladly.

I won't soon forget Zanzibar, the Indian Ocean island just off Dar Es Salaam. One quaint hotel on the entire island with magnificent hammered Arabic brass on the huge wooden doors. Little bamboo curtains inside. A 12 inch lizard fell off the ceiling right into our mashed potatoes.

So help me, there was a guy in a fez wearing dark glasses across the street, always watching the hotel door from behind a newspaper. He looked exactly like Peter Lorre. I expected Sidney Greenstreet to walk through the door at any time, and Humphrey Bogart to bail us out of trouble.

I'm thinking, this is it. I've seen Victoria Falls while its Zambezi River was at flood stage, Mount Kiliminjaro, Mombassa, and now the mysterious Zanzibar. I'm feeling smug. I've been around.

Then another tour group showed up. They just blew in from Timbuktu!

Which reminds me of a gentleman named Guy Purvis from Harmony, Minnesota. He was a retired farmer—never married—with nothing to do with his money but travel. He was a quaint old curmudgeon who'd been everywhere—except the Soviet Union. That's where our paths first crossed when I was hosting a WCCO Radio Good Neighbor Tour.

Guy fell asleep in the Bolshoi Theatre in Moscow. We barely rescued him before they locked up the joint for the night.

He didn't like Russian beer. Nobody did. He didn't like Russian Vodka—had tasted better white lightning back during prohibition. He didn't like genuine Beluga caviar—too salty. He wasn't even impressed by the gold and bejeweled carraiges of the Tsars and Tsarinas—"Too heavy! I got a better hay rack. Think of them poor horses." He liked the ballet better than the opera, because you didn't have any Russian words to cope with.

Guy Purvis went along on our tour through Africa. But I must backtrack here to set the stage.

After that fabulous Eastern Europe and Soviet tour my waggish brother-in-law started riding me. He had somehow managed a college education from Luther College in Decorah, Iowa. He said, "If you really want to take a tour you should lead one to the homecoming game between Spillville and Protivin, Iowa which Spillville always wins 7 to 6. You can take a side trip to see the famous Billy clocks."

It seems there's this museum full of cuckoo clocks carved by these two brothers. They all go off at the same time. It's bedlam at noon and midnight. I dismissed it as a hoax.

I was to learn later that there really is a museum—quite famous—and the brothers name was Biely, not pronounced "billy."

Back to Guy Purvis. As we took in the wonders of Uganda, Tanzania, Kenya, Zambia, Rhodesia, Zanzibar, South Africa.

Ultimately we found ourselves at the base of Mount Kilimanjaro. We were protected from animals by a wooden stockade refuge—again, right out of a Tarzan movie. A huge bonfire burned in a hollowed-out rock as we sipped cocktails. Kilimanjaro was magnificent as the weather cooperated and the sun turned the snowy peak to a rosey hue.

I was in heaven! I'd arrived! Hemingway must have been sitting right here when he wrote his famous novel.

Then out of the corner of my ear, I hear Guy Purvis say to another tour member, "Well, it's pretty all right, but if you really want to see something you gotta see the billy clocks in Spillville, Iowa."

Right then I decided. One day I'll be driving in Iowa and spot a sign saying, "Biely Clock Museum—2 miles ➡."

Forgive me Spillville, I'm gonna tear the sign down.

## IN AND OUT OF RUSSIA

Those WCCO Radio Good Neighbor trips could be harrowing. That marvelous Soviet and Eastern European trip was so popular, we sold two planeloads. I hosted the first group into the Soviet Union for two weeks, then departed Kiev for Prague in Czechoslovakia. The second group was behind us hosted by Gordon Mikkelson.

The plan was for me to double back from Prague and switch hosting duties with Mikkelson, who would fly ahead to finish the tour with group number one.

On a Saturday night, I return to the Moscow airport alone and the customs agent declared I did not have a visa to enter the Soviet Union.

I protest that I'm supposed to have one, and produce a travel agent letter in English listing me as having visas for returning to Russia and re-entering Czechoslovakia. That cut no ice with the Soviet border police. They hauled out a short, stout border cop who spoke very little English. He declared, "No Visa—back to Praha (Prague) you go!" Then he orders me off to the slammer, since the next Prague flight is at 9 a.m. the next day. I managed to get a short reprieve and phoned the U.S. Embassy. We decided that some Red Army lummox in Leningrad had ripped off all my extra visas with those of the other passengers upon our arrival. That Leningrad arrival was imposing. These Red Army guys just marched down the airplane aisle and collected everyone's passport. We didn't see them again for more than an hour and not until we reached our hotel.

Anyway, the embassy guy said, "Just keep telling them you're a tour leader and maybe they won't kick you out of the country."

He promised to contact the Kremlin the next morning for an emergency visa. The trouble was the Big K didn't open until 9 a.m. when I'm supposed to be booted out.

He said, "Sometimes somebody shows up early. Just keep telling them you're a tour leader!"

The short, stout border cop confiscates my visa-less passport and sends me on a one-mile forced march to the slammer, which is actually locked dormitories of the Soviet's Intourist facility. Your room is not locked but each floor is. Naturally, I'm on the third floor and my luggage weighed a ton.

The room was the size of a large closet, the bed not much better than a cot. There's a locker room type shower down the hall which I stroll into about 8:30 the next morning. I figure the more I drag my feet, the better chance I have of getting help from my Embassy and the dreaded Kremlin.

There was a guy shaving in the shower room who appeared to be of Middle East nationality. My cheery, "Good Morning," sent him packing in fear.

So, I'm showering and humming and whistling—anything to buy time—when the floor monitor stomps in, hammers on the wall and indicates in a flood of Russian that I must hurry.

Well, we make it back to the huge Moscow airport shortly before 9 a.m. and there stands that same cop (must have worked all night) holding my passport.

He barks, "Visa?"

I answer, "Intourist," nodding toward the Intourist office where the phone is.

He bellows, "Spreken Deutch!"

I answer, "Englais."

He yells, "Praha!"

I answer, "Intourist."

He grabs my suitcase and pulls, saying "Praha!"

I let go and the suitcase hits him on the toe. I know it hurt. I just started toward the Intourist office with the short, stout border cop following, lugging my suitcase and turning bright red as he babbles in unintelligible Russian.

At the Intourist office, he gets into an argument with the Intourist staffers, all of whom speak excellent English. One of the staff nudges me, and secretly gives me an OK sign (finger and thumb forming a circle). I understand only when the PA system switches from Russian to English announcing the departure of the 9 a.m. flight to Prague. The Intourist staffers are in the business of getting people into Russia, the border cop's job is to keep people out. The two agencies don't see eye to eye.

At any rate, I'm given until noon to get a visa, or back to Prague I go on the noon flight.

It took the Kremlin until 11:30 to notify us that an emergency visa would be provided for 25 American dollars.

When an Intourist staffer escorted me to border police headquarters, the short, stout cop was still on duty. We're talking 16 or 17 hours after my first meeting with him, and he's still got my passport clutched in his fat little paw.

The Intourist staffer explains the visa arrangement and the cop launches into a blistering Russian tirade. The Intourist guy says, "That was meant expressly for you!"

I said, "Great! Tell him I don't understand a word he's saying."

The staffer says, "It's just as well you don't; he swears a lot. In brief, he says nobody gets into the Soviet Union without a visa, and this will never happen again."

I said, "Tell him that's okay by me—Spaseba—Dasvadanya!" That means, "Thank you and Goodby," the only Russian I know to this day.

Talk about a beauracracy. My $25 was transported to the Kremlin by taxi and my visa returned by the same method, a process that consumed the rest of the day, almost six hours.

That was okay though, because I got to know the guys at Intourist. I helped one guy translate an English idiom into Russian. It was a slangy expression he didn't understand. Oh yes, it came from a letter I noted being sent from someone in the Soviet Union to someone in London. In their spare time, these Intourist multi-linguists opened and translated (censored) mail.

I discovered that Moscow had a law: No public heat until mid-October (which had not quite arrived.) The Intourist staff had an illegal electric heater they were using. Every so often a lookout would signal, and the heater would be hidden away quickly as some official stepped into the office. My new friend gestured as these people left saying, "100 percent Communist!"

Outside the office was a bank of telephone booths. I was anxious to keep tabs on the fate of our Minnesota Twins who were locked in a race for the pennant with the Boston Red Sox. Our tour members expected their leaders to run this information down whenever possible. English newspapers were several days late.

The Intourist office phone was no longer available to me—certainly not for such trivial information. But the staff allowed me out of the office to use the pay phone. It cost me one American dollar to buy about 25 cents worth of kopek coins.

All but one of the phone booths was locked, and those had no windows. The pay phone was unlocked and did have a window. My first few tries to ring up the CBS correspondent in Moscow ran afoul of busy signals. As I waited on a nearby bench, I noticed someone approach one of the locked phone booths and knock. It opened, and the two switched places. I saw it happen three times. Those phone booths were nothing more than taps, manned by personnel monitoring calls from who knows where.

I finally connected with the CBS number and got a heavily-accented voice in response. I asked for the correspondent by name, got some gobbledygook in return— and a quick hang-up. I think I'd been intercepted by one of those locked phone booths. That night, after finally reaching my hotel, I tried again from my room phone.

The line went dead and never came back to life.

I used an old James Bond trick (hair placed across my suitcase) to determine that my luggage was searched daily when I was away. I even discovered that someone was taking nips out of my meager supply of Canadian Club whenever I was absent.

The Union of Soviet Socialist Republics of 1967 is long since history. For those of us growing up during the Cold War, it's mind boggling to witness the sudden change of what was iron-fisted communism.

I read today that Russia is plagued with crime of Mafia proportions. In 1967 I witnessed a Moscow citizen race to catch an electric trolley in the middle of a busy street. In so doing, he "jaywalked," thereby breaking the law. A non-uniformed Soviet policeman (there were lots of them) raced to the trolley, stopped it, boarded it and forcefully removed the offender. The force was such that the man's arm was broken. I heard it snap, and the grimace of pain on the man's face was obvious. This for "jaywalking!" How many jaywalkers do you see everyday in our country even though we have the same regulations.

I also read today that Soviets are returning to religion. In 1967, virtually all Russian Orthodox churches had been turned into museums. The State did not recognize religion. Religion was merely tolerated as "superstition." Some worship was allowed for the sake of the "old people."

One of our tour members was born in Russia. He was Jewish. He recruited several of us to try to find a synagogue, reportedly located in downtown Moscow.

After many years away, he still could speak passable Russian, so he directed our cab to the area. With some difficulty, we found the synagogue. It was small, seedy and run-down.

More importantly, it was closed! This happened to be a Saturday—the Hebrew Sabbath! Our tour member tried to converse with some bearded Soviets who looked for all the world like Rabbis. He tried Russian, he tried Hebrew, but he was ignored. It wasn't until he turned to us and spoke in English, that one of the Rabbis approached and talked to him. Once our man spoke English, they knew he was a tourist and not the KGB.

He asked why the Synagogue was closed and the Rabbi painted a dreary picture. It was almost impossible to practice Judaism because you couldn't practice any religion and still belong to the Communist Party. No Party membership—no job! It was that simple.

Our tour group visited Zgorsk, the seat of the Russian Orthodox Church, some 60 kilometers north of Moscow. It was a marvelous walled city, strewn with almost a dozen magnificent, multi-spired cathedrals. Only one was operative. It was headquarters for a struggling Russian Orthodox Seminary. We saw a scattering of bearded priests-to-be striding to and from the churches.

Our guide was a multi-lingual woman from the Ukraine—the Soviet Breadbasket and home of many Jews before Communism. Guide jobs were Communistic plums frequently awarded by the State to Soviet athletic stars. Our guide happened to be a Silver Medal Olympic swimmer. She also happened to have come from a Ukrainian Jewish family. She admitted this, but also admitted having renounced her faith.

"Just superstition," she said, echoing the Party line.

At one point, she led our group into the cathedral. She showed us priceless religious icons. There were dozens, hung on various walls. Many were centuries old. As we moved around at her directions, we couldn't help but notice a small group knelt before the altar. A Russian Orthodox priest was conducting a service. The group was all elderly—obviously peasants.

Our guide remarked that she didn't understand why these peasants would save for years and then spend their life savings for a pilgramage to Zgorsk.

Then after describing another icon, she told us to follow her as she strode right through the ongoing religious service. Her path placed her between the small congregation and the priest.

None of us followed.

In a loud voice she said, "This way please!"

None of us moved.

She remained planted there, trying to get us to follow. The priest just stood silent. The worshipers remained on their knees, hardly looking up.

I couldn't stand it. I beckoned her away from the altar, and explained in a whisper that there was no way this group of Americans was going to interrupt a worship service of any faith.

She merely shrugged and led us around the back of the church, but she never lowered her voice. She completely ignored the service as she delivered her guide's spiel.

Before leaving Zgorsk, we were allowed to meet the head of the Seminary in his small office. He spoke rather good English. We spoke of his obvious difficulties in the Soviet system. He skirted many questions, but tried to be amicable. His eyes darted frequently to our guide.

One tour member asked if we could donate to the Seminary. He indicated a typical church collection plate at the rear of the room, but insisted he do something in return, whereupon he produced a stack of hardback books describing the history of the Russian Orthodox Religion. They were printed in English, and marvelously illustrated in color.

I can't estimate how much money our group piled in that collection plate, but I didn't see anything under a $20 bill, and they were all American dollars.

During our return to Moscow, several of us wound up in a lenghty discussion with our guide—a discussion about religion in general, its place in the Soviet Union and in the world. It was sometimes tense, as our guide clung to her atheistic stand.

But when all the others had deboarded the bus, she quietly asked me if she could have one of the books the priest had handed out. I gave her mine.

Now comes the windup of this unusual story.

More than one year later, I recieved a strange piece of mail. The envelope was battered and torn. The address was hardly legible. Some of it was obliterated by postmarks in various languages. To this day, I'm amazed it reached me because the address was far from correct. The most I could make out was "Chapman—WCCO—Minnisote— America." Thank God for good old 'CCO. If it says WCCO and anything close to Minnesota, it'll probably get here.

The envelope contained an Easter card. It was not exactly a Hallmark, but it had a dove and an olive branch—even a cross on it.

It was from our Soviet guide.

Even though she spoke English rather well, she didn't write it too hot.

In handwriting, her cryptic message read:

"Mr. Chapman, Happy Easter to you. I hope you well. It seems what we talked about may be real. I thank you for the book." Then her signature.

Looking back on that bus discussion, I remembered the anguished look in her eyes as she dueled with her tormentors. She seemed especially frustrated when our Jewish tour member leaned hard on her Hebrew heritage.

I've re-read her message several times. She didn't say much, but I'm sure she regained her long lost faith. How long it took—for that matter how long the card was in the global mail—I'll never know.

Such was the Soviet Union in 1967.

## DELIGHTFUL EASTERN EUROPE

Leaving Russia for Czechoslovakia was like coming out of a Gulag. It was on a Czech airliner—much more refined than the Aeroflot Soviet aircraft. It even featured pretty Czech flight attendants who smiled and acted cheerful. The flight happened to contain more than a dozen Czech businessmen who had spent a month in Russia on some training venture.

Aeroflot service gives passengers nothing but mineral water and hard candies.

Suddenly, two stewardesses swept down the aisle carrying genuine Czechoslovakian beer—only the best in the world. The roar from the Czech businessmen was deafening.

"Ah—Pilsner Peevo—Ah, Pilsner!"

These guys, like me, had spent a month in Russia, with only Muskva Peevo (Moscow Beer) available. I have drunk beer all over the world. To me beer rates from excellent on up—with the sole exception of Muskva Peevo—worst beer in the world.

Which brings me to another hilarious anecdote.

Prague, Czechoslovakia, is one of the gem cities of Europe. We were there at a time when the Czechs were enjoying economic boom times—and drifting slowly but relentlessly out of the Soviet "Iron Curtain." Just weeks after our departure the Soviet Union invaded Czechoslovakia with tanks and troops to oust the "western leaning" Czech President—and quash the satellite country's bent for freedom and Democracy.

But our Czech stay was delightful, including a trip of about 30 kilometers to a town called Carlstein, site of a travel-poster type castle built on the edge of a towering mountain top.

We had to switch to a very small bus to manipulate the narrow, curving mountain road to the castle. It was harrowing going up—double that coming down. Atop the mountain, some 100 yards from the chalet itself, was a turn-around cul-de-sac where stood a quaint, rustic mountain chalet with a small cobblestone patio outside.

The patio had chairs and tables placed right beside two huge wood beer kegs, mounted into the side of the mountain cliff. There was a natural spring seeping from the cliff. The Czechs had dug into the rock and hollowed out space for the beer kegs, keeping the beer expertly chilled. This was real pilsner on tap. The town of Pilsen itself (birthplace of Pilsner) was only 15 more kilometers down the road.

Well, the castle was magnificent, but a handful of us said, "You people go ahead. We'll wait here and catch you on the way back."

A castle is a castle is a castle, but pilsner is something else—especially in that setting.

We discovered that a full pint stein of genuine pilsner drawn from those imposing barrels cost us two Czech Crowns per mug. That figured out to about eight cents American. Needless to say, we downed a few.

Which brought me to a point where I had to visit the men's room.

Without our translator, I entered the chalet. It was gorgeous. Huge, rustic wooden beams—everything you'd ever expect from a genuine mountain chalet. I managed to indicate my needs to the bartender who directed me through a gigantic wooden and brass door into a toilet facility as rustic as everything else in the joint—with one exception!

There on the rustic wooden wall was a gleaming, porcelain American Standard urinal. I think they're made somewhere in Wisconsin. It stood out like a sore thumb—so out of place with the rest of the decor.

"How unique," I thought, as I stepped up to do my business. I'm glancing at the rustic ceiling beams when I seem to hear water running. Water was running!

On closer examination, I discovered that the chalet featured gleaming American Standard urinals—but there was no plumbing. The down spout from the urinal merely hung in mid air—directing deposits into a groove in the floor which flowed neatly out through the wall and down the mountainside.

I was pissing on my own shoes.

Upon my return to the patio, I kept my face as straight as possible when I told my cohorts, "I don't know if you have to go, but it's probably a smart idea to hit the "John" before we start back down the mountain."

They've never forgotten.

### BENNYHOFF

One of my favorite associates in the WCCO Radio newsroom was Gary Bennyhoff.

Gary was an accomplished writer and reporter, but also a close fishing and hunting buddy. He and I were among the original founders of Muskies, Inc.

St. Paul muskie addict Gil Hamm gathered about a dozen similar muskie nuts together at the old Criterion Restaurant in St. Paul's Midway. He proposed the idea and we all agreed to pitch in. However, I remember

## IF YOU'RE TOO BUSY TO FISH, YOU'RE TOO BUSY!

That's not bait. It's a fish **Dick Chapman** caught.

**Barbara Chapman** often outfishes **Dick**. (10 lb. Northern)

But not always. (5 lb. Walleye)

**Barbara** landed a 3 inch trout.

telling Gil Hamm, "We may be tilting at windmills. It's a whale of an undertaking."

I underestimated the exuberance of Gil Hamm.

He infected all of us. He goaded us into monumental promotional activities, and before you knew it we had 400 members. Today there are nearly 50 Chapters in more than a dozen states and Canada.

In the past 30 years, the growth and success of Muskies, Inc. has been phenomonal. Members donated money for fish purchases, volunteered time for rearing and stocking, badgered the Department of Natural Resources to abolish outmoded rearing and stocking techniques, and introduced the concept that will go down in history as the Muskies, Inc. legacy—"Catch and Release!"

Muskies, Inc. members today release more than 95 percent of their fish. The same is true of many non-members. The concept has spread to other species, like walleye, bass, even trout and panfish. With big females allowed to live and spawn anew, the quality of our fishery can improve constantly, insuring the sport for future generations.

I started this chapter about "the crazy stuff." Well, Bennyhoff was involved in something real crazy.

An inmate escaped from the Anoka State Hospital one night. Authorities described him as mentally unstable, armed and dangerous. In fact, the escapee had vowed not to be taken alive and threatened to kill any lawmen he encountered.

WCCO Radio, like all the media, duly reported the manhunt each day. One evening, the escapee telephoned our newsroom and Bennyhoff happened upon the call. As Assistant News Director, I was on duty too. Bennyhoff signaled me as soon as he realized who was on the phone.

"Keep him talking," I said, "We'll trace the call."

Let me tell you—that's easier said than done. Through our switchboard, I talked to any number of operators and telephone supervisors trying to trace that call. I cross-connected police and telephone personnel. I begged. I pleaded.

All the while (seemed like hours) Bennyhoff is struggling to keep the fugitive on the line. At one point he yelled, "Chapman! This guy is threatening to come down here and kill me! Hurry up!"

It seems the reason for this wierdo's call was that he resented being described as mentally unstable. Bennyhoff later quoted him as saying, "I'm not crazy! And if you don't put that on the air, I'm gonna come down there and shoot you!"

The episode concluded with a successful phone trace and the fugitive's apprehension without a shot being fired.

Bennyhoff was nonetheless edgy about answering phones for some time afterwards.

Gary and I also found ourselves in the vanguard of the snowmobile explosion. I remember our first test ride on the early Skidoos, down an alley behind Ostrom's Sporting Goods Store on East Lake Street. It was Fall and there wasn't any snow, but we tried them out on gravel just the same.

When Winter did arrive, Ray Ostrom bought some time on WCCO Radio to advertise his plan to offer free test rides on his Skidoos on the ice of Lake Minnetonka's Brown's Bay.

Someone, perhaps General Manager Larry Haeg, was innovative enough to make it a big deal. Why not a full afternoon's broadcast regarding all Winter activities? Chapman and Bennyhoff wound up doing several hours live broadcasting on both Saturday and Sunday afternoon. We chatted with ice fishermen, ice-boaters, ice skaters, sledding fanatics—

whatever.

But it was the snowmobiles that drew all the attention. The sport's time had arrived. Thousands showed up for a quick spin. Since Ostrom had fewer than a dozen Skidoos, it meant people lined up for hours awaiting their turns. It also created a massive traffic jam on County Road 15. At times the slowdown stretched for miles—all the way from Brown's Bay to Wayzata eastward and past Navarre westward. Police from several communities turned out to direct the cars. They were not too happy with us. Heck, it wasn't our fault. Who could have anticipated such a turnout?

Right in the middle of all this bedlam, I glanced out over the lake to see a huge, colorful hot-air balloon drifting toward us. Wind conditions were perfect, and the pilot could hold his altitude wherever he wanted. The pilot happened to be Tracy Anderson, world-class balloonist.

We outfitted Bennyhoff with a microphone and about 100 yards of mike cord.

He slogged out there through the snow and conducted a dynamite interview with the balloonist. Bennyhoff actually strolled alongside the balloon which the pilot held at a mere two feet off the ice. You could hear the hot air blasts as the pilot deftly maintained his course. It was great radio—and wouldn't you know it—nobody had a camera.

# THE UNFORGETTABLES

After forty years in this business of broadcast journalism, the list of unforgettable characters you've met is substantial.

**Colonel Sanders**, founder of the Kentucky Fried Chicken empire is one. Man what a hustler! But don't shake his hand—it's greasy.

The late **Lem Karcher** of Ortonville, Minnesota, is another. His son Jim worked with me in the 'CCO newsroom. It was Jim who talked his dad into advertising Hobo Soup on 'CCO with me as the spokesman. The senior Karcher had spent a portion of his life as a genuine hobo—riding the rails nationwide. After settling down to become a prosperous small town daily newspaper publisher (The Ortonville Independent), he put together his own canning company to make Hobo Soup. Lem claimed it was a bean and broth concoction he learned in the hobo jungles of America. The damn stuff tasted pretty good and the company flourished for some time. The Ortonville Independent, under Jim's guidance, remains one of Minnesota's best.

**Minnesota Viking Hall of Famer Fran Tarkenton** is one.

Coach Van Brocklin in the early years would say, "He's gonna take you 20 yards, either forward or backward." Fran delighted in making the back-East media big-shot reporters wait their turn for interviews until he had satisfied local reporters like myself.

**Vikings Jim Marshall and Matt Blair** had the most magnificently proportioned bodies I've ever seen (and I've seen them locker-room naked on many occasions). Both had tremendous shoulders with tiny (Lil' Abner) waists.

**Viking Hall of Famer Alan Page.** Arguably, he was the finest defensive lineman in history. My wife and I played occasional bridge games with him and his wife, Diane. His card sense nowhere near matched his athletic prowess or his determined reasoning.

Page refused the coaching staff's constant urging to add more weight. He had better use for his legs in later years. And you must admire the man's devotion to students for constantly proding them to put education ahead of athletics during school years. As a Minnesota Supreme Court Justice, he's a true role model.

**Academy Award Winner Lee Marvin** ("Cat Ballou"). We met at the Minnesota Press Club as he downed some cocktails and griped about Director Elia Kazan passing him by for the role of the Allied prosecutor in the movie "Judgement at Nuremberg." Marvin claimed he was perfect for the part, but Kazan "played the star game" and selected Richard Widmark instead. A year later Marvin won his Oscar.

**The Wild Bunch at KSTP. Bob Ryan, Dick Nesbitt, Johnny Morris, Jim McGovern, Bill McGivern and Eric Renwahl.** They were a bunch of hard-driving newsies under the tutelage of News Director **Bud Meier**. Meier is a piece of work himself. He hired a psychic to find the missing body of St. Paul mobster Rocky Lupino. All the guy found was a shovel, but Channel 5 milked it for days.

Bud Meier learned that convicted murderer T. Eugene Thompson fancied himself as a good "piano bar" singer and planned to perform in a variety show at Stillwater State Prison. Thompson, a St. Paul lawyer with a mistress, was convicted for hiring a murderer to slay his wife after he had doubled her life insurance.

Anyway, Meier sent a crew to the prison performance and filmed Thompson singing the love ballad "When I Fall In Love—It Will Be Forever." Then it was aired on Channel 5's 10 p.m. News, complete with superimposed footage of Mrs. Thompson's bloodied body being hauled from the crime scene on a coroner's gurney. I'm told Channel 5's boss Stanley Hubbard, Jr. was furious, but company founder Stanley Hubbard, Sr. thought the piece was hilarious.

**Dave Moore** of WCCO-TV. In 1957, CBS refused to let Walter Cronkite out of his contract to become Channel 4's news anchor. Dave Moore was a virtual walk-on off the street. He was an actor, not a reporter. But it didn't take him long to teach himself how to become a reporter. Yet his acting heritage allowed him to insert his incomparable personality into his broadcasts. The man is a natural at injecting casualness into his delivery, then suddenly turning serious and authoritative. His eye contact is so genuine, you'd think he was in the middle of your living room.

Some years ago, his Saturday night "Bedtime Newz" at midnight was the freshest spoof of TV journalism ever put together. Dave's comedy genius was the backbone of a broadcast that had viewers interrupting parties or keeping people awake past their normal retirement hour. Few know that Dave, personally, spent the better part of 24 hours putting that masterpiece together. Sadly, it became physically impossible to continue the grind.

Dave ignored many serious overtures to move to bigger markets or the network. He said, simply, "My act won't play there." Dave knew his territory.

My hat is forever off to him.

# Proclamation

**WHEREAS:**     Dick Chapman has been a leader in news broadcasting in Minnesota and the region for nearly four decades; and

**WHEREAS:**     Dick Chapman has contributed to Minnesota's environmental quality of life by co-founding Muskies, Incorporated, a catch and release program that has become a model for the nation; and

**WHEREAS:**     Dick Chapman has lent his time and services to a variety of causes, including the Multiple Sclerosis Society; and

**WHEREAS:**     Dick Chapman has informed and entertained millions of WCCO listeners across the Midwest in a variety of ways, from his "Honest to Goodness" quiz program to Governors' fishing openers to his Peabody award-winning coverage of weather disasters in our area; and

**WHEREAS:**     Dick Chapman, the avid angler, has served as role model for Grumpy Old Men everywhere;

NOW THEREFORE, I, ARNE H. CARLSON, Governor of the State of Minnesota, do hereby proclaim Friday, December 22, 1995 to be

## D I C K     C H A P M A N     D A Y

in Minnesota, to honor Minnesota's truly "Good Neighbor".

IN WITNESS WHEREOF, I have hereunto set my hand and caused the Great Seal of the State of Minnesota to be affixed at the State Capitol this twenty-second day of December in the year of our Lord one thousand nine hundred and ninety-five, and of the State the one hundred thirty-seventh.

_Arne H. Carlson_
GOVERNOR

_Joan A. Growe_
SECRETARY OF STATE

**MINNESOTA GOV. CARLSON'S** Proclamation surprised **Chappy.**

# WCCO —THEN AND NOW

In Meredith Wilson's famous musical "The Music Man," the opening showstopper features a group of traveling salesmen on a train expounding the prowess of one Professor Harold Hill who sells musical instruments to small town high schools in order to create a boys' band. Keeps them out of pool halls. We all know pool halls spell "trouble." That sequence ends with the salesmen agreeing, in our business—"Ya gotta know the territory!"

The people guiding WCCO Radio in the '60s, '70s and '80s certainly knew the territory. And what a territory it was—and still is.

"Minnesota Nice" is not some catchword dreamt up by a columnist or adman. There really is a Minnesota Nice. It's the people. Yes, we're loaded with Scandinavians, Germans, and ethnic whatevers—but most of them seem at peace with where they live and know how best to live here. That means coping with a winter that horrifies sunbelters. It means being a good neighbor, which for a long time was the motto of WCCO Radio, "Good Neighbor to the Northwest."

That used to drive News Director Jim Bormann wild because we're not really "Northwest," we're upper midwest. Trouble was, the StarTribune had already staked a claim to "Upper Midwest." There was a time when we just referred to our territory as "CCO-Land." It made a lot of sense since the signal stretches from Minot to Menomonie and from Des Moines to

Dryden (that's in Ontario).

At any rate, management came from within. They knew the territory. One of the most successful General Managers was Larry Haeg, a one-time state legislator, who worked his way up from 'CCO's Farm Director. He once said, "The best way to manage the talent at 'CCO Radio is to keep your hands off them."

All he did was steer a little. Let them have their head. Yes, he'd toss in some innovations. He might dress somebody down. But mostly he let the creative juices flow.

If Maynard Speece let fly with a raw joke in the early mornings, Haeg would haul him back to his office for a rebuke. But he'd admit the joke was funny. He used to admonish Speece and Roger Erickson with, "Remember, even before 6 a.m. it's 'teats' we refer to—not the other word."

Larry Haeg looked upon WCCO-TV as the enemy—the competition, just like the StarTribune. Nevermind it was all the same company with the newspaper holding 49 percent of the stock. Curiously, Haeg ended up as president of the whole outfit before he was through.

It was Haeg's idea to mount a massive relief effort for Colfax, Wisconsin, when it was smashed by a tornado. That's doing things right.

When WCCO Radio captured the prestigious Peabody Award in 1965, the station presented every single employee with a silverplate copy of the Peabody trophy.

It was Haeg's idea to honor a WCCO Radio Good Neighbor every weekday morning at 8 o'clock. He also wanted me to create a "Day in History" segment for what would be called "The Morning Almanac." What an assignment. I can't tell you the number of hours spent going through newspaper files to dig up a day-by-day chronological history.

I also can't tell you the trials and tribulations of coming up with a

# Good Neighbor
## AWARD

### *Dick Chapman*

*We have a very "special" WCCO Radio Good Neighbor Award today...*
*as we honor the man who for so many years was the "voice" of the*
*WCCO Radio Good Neighbor. He began his career at WCCO Radio in*
*1957, a young journalist who wrote copy for legendary newscaster*
*Cedric Adams. Over the next four decades he, himself, became a*
*broadcasting giant throughout the upper Midwest. He also lent his*
*talents to various causes, such as the Multiple Sclerosis Society, and*
*to conservation programs, including "Muskies Incorporated," of*
*which he is a founding member. Congratulations to today's*
*WCCO Radio Good Neighbor, one of our distinguished alumni...*
*Dick Chapman!*

*December 22, 1995*
Date

WCCO Radio General Manager

**ANOTHER SURPRISE!**

Good Neighbor six days every week. Since late 1962, WCCO Radio has named more than 60,000 Good Neighbors.

The very first WCCO Radio Good Neighbor (Dec. 29, 1962) was General Lauris Norstad, Commander of NATO, and a native of Red Wing, Minnesota.

For more than 25 years, I hunted down Good Neighbors—some famous, some hardly known. They ranged from movers and shakers in various communities, to the simple cab driver who took it upon himself to carry fresh roses in his cab for presentations to ladies apparently stressed out by the rat race of the day.

Each Good Neighbor was lauded on the air and presented with a certificate suitable for framing.

There were times I really had to scrape to find someone. There were other times when I had too many candidates to squeeze in.

Listeners nominated lots of candidates and usually wanted the broadcast on a certain day, which was not always possible. In some of those cases I've been offered bribes (never accepted). In several cases, I've been threatened. Nobody ever threw a punch. I'm quick on my feet and subscribe to Lord Falstaff's famed philosophy that "discretion is the better part of valor."

Time never permitted thorough investigation of some Good Neighbor candidates. It was embarrassing, on an occasion or two, to honor a Good Neighbor who had died before the broadcast made the air.

It was also embarrassing for a no-goodnik to send me a Good Neighbor who just happened to be running for School Board (a fact excluded in the nominating letter). An opponent complained. I had to hustle up equal time. Thank goodness neither person won.

But with this lack of control, I lived in fear that someone would send me a flowery description of someone who looked like a natural—only to find it was actually a mass-murderer in Stillwater State Prison.

Neverthless, the WCCO Radio Good Neighbor Award became a coveted honor. It was also a great marketing tool for sponsors, and what 'CCO P.R. Director Rob Brown called the greatest public relations gimmick ever invented.

Each Good Neighbor certificate included congratulations from the current sponsors of the program. There were the sponsors' names, hanging in a frame behind the recipients desk. Recipients would write me thank-you notes actually asking me to pass the thanks on to the program's sponsors (Northland Ford Dealers; Northwestern Bank; there were others).

But the real benefit—a 'CCO Radio bonanza—was the fact that every community newspaper throughout 'CCO-land would carry a story about Good Neighbor winners if they came from their area. Sometimes it would be front page and include a photograph of the local WCCO Radio Good Neighbor. Is that public relations? Rob Brown said, "No one could afford to buy that exposure."

WCCO Radio sponsored free dance parties for kids attending the High School basketball tournaments. It sure kept them from mischief in the hotels.

The station got its personalties out and about participating in small town pageants and parades, or whatever was happening to put a face with the voice. That's doing things right.

It was my idea to create the WCCO Radio Fishing Opener. Haeg had the foresight to approve it.

That annual springtime ritual saw millions of anglers hitting the water for the elusive walleye and northern pike in mid-May. It marked the end of "cabin fever." Winter was over. The good times are here.

WCCO had been paying slight attention to such a momentous occurrence. A few staffers, lots of salesmen, and department heads would swap a free weekend at Izaty's Resort on Lake Mille Lacs for a couple of mentions on the air.

I convinced Haeg that there was a very saleable package there. We expanded the opening weekend broadcasts to dozens of reports each day. We moved our talent to choice resort locations and involved whole cities in the promotions. The Alexandrias, Brainerds, Detroit Lakes, Park Rapids, Willmars—you name them—were lined up on a list requesting the right to host the 'CCO Radio Fishing Opener.

I invited Governors to join us, and they did. (The first was Orville Freeman.) It was excellent free time for a politician. Even non-fishermen like Elmer L. Anderson took advantage of the invitation.

Gov. Karl Rolvaag, an ardent angler, realized he could do the same thing to promote Minnesota as a vacation destination. And so the Governor's Fishing Opener was born—almost an exact copy of 'CCO's. The Governors would invite outdoor media folks from all over the state and the nation. The response has been tremendous.

Gov. Wendell Anderson got his face and accompanying fish on the cover of Time magazine during one of those openers.

Wisconsin Governor Warren Knowles jumped aboard and copied what Rolvaag had done for his state. The opening ritual is just as big in Wisconsin. I attended Gov. Knowles' first opening. Ironically I attended his last, 25 years later. The former Governor collapsed and died as he came off a lake on opening day.

**DICK CHAPMAN** passing his hat to **GOV. TOMMY THOMPSON**.

The **GUV** even
agreed to a swap.

I'll never forget that first one, though. Gov. Knowles had invited Gov. Rolvaag of Minnesota and Gov. Harold Hughes of Iowa. Rolvaag declined, but Hughes accepted.

Warren Knowles enjoyed his booze. Gov. Hughes was an outspoken recovered alcoholic.

It came to pass that I arranged a live telephone broadcast-interview with both Governors to go into the Noontime News. The only suitable phone I could find was in a pay booth, designed for the use of one person. But the three of us (Hughes was a big guy) crammed into that booth. I won't say that Gov. Knowles was tipsy, but his breath left little doubt he had imbibed something from the world of spirits. Gov. Hughes was obviously distressed during the entire interview. For my part, I was happy to get out of that booth alive.

During a more recent Wisconsin opener, Governor Tommy Thompson spoke at a media dinner and wise-cracked about nearby Minnesota bragging about 10-thousand lakes. He said, "Wisconsin has lakes with fish in them."

During that evening, locals presented Gov. Thompson with various gifts. I stepped forward and butted into the program to present the Governor with my WCCO Radio hat. I said something like, "I think you should know that WCCO Radio covers more of your state than any Wisconsin station does. Besides, Minnesotans know how to catch fish."

It was a pretty funny put down. Gov. Thompson handled it well, saying, "I wouldn't have bad-mouthed Minnesota if I had known someone was here representing a station that covers that much of Wisconsin."

Nonetheless, WCCO Radio's innovation of the Fishing Opener was doing things right. The concept was expanded to the Bass Opener, Pheasant Hunting Opener (really big when we had some birds), the Deer

Opener, the Duck Opener, even the Snowmobile Opener. They got 'CCO out and about.

Following the disastrous tornadoes of May 6, 1965, it became obvious we should do whatever possible to hone and polish our severe weather capabilities. We needed eyes on the sky.

The station's innovative P.R. man, Rob Brown, and I took on the task of roaming the Metro area looking for high spots. We conscripted listeners to be our constant eyes on the sky. We even climbed atop the Foshay Tower to determine if a "lookout location" could be installed there. We can say from personal experience it was too dangerous. But we had the Metro covered—a grid of sky-watchers, happy to help.

But what about the rest of the state? You can't just concentrate on the Twin Cities. And what about Wisconsin, the Dakotas and Iowa?.

Rob and I, with Larry Haeg's blessing, turned to Minnesota's AAA, the American Automobile Association. We devised an area-wide network of weather reporters comprised of AAA service station managers and the vast army of AAA travel agents and insurance salesmen throughout our region. It was great public relations for the AAA people and a perfect system for WCCO Radio. We dubbed it "Direct Line." Each AAA person had an ID card with several phone numbers that could put them on the air in moments.

It turned out to be a bonanza during incoming snowstorms, as well as heavy thunderstorms and tornadoes. Chief Meteorologist Joe Strube told me his forecasters listened to our AAA people constantly. He said, "My budget can't buy so many weather reporters." Strube even set up weather watching instructions for our AAA Army. Why the system is now defunct is beyond me. Too many cooks spoil the broth, they say. Management changed, and none of the new bosses adhered to the old bromide, "If it ain't broke, don't fix it." Quite frankly, the new brass didn't know the territory.

WCCO Radio's more recent bosses fired then-St. Paul Pioneer Press Columnist Bill Farmer because the manager at the time "didn't like his voice."

Never mind that he was one of the best humorists to come down the pike in years and listeners were warming to his parlays with Roger Erickson. Farmer is one of those guys who just thinks funny.

Example: Roger brought up a story about a farm mare who gave birth to a zebra, opining that it must have been "one of those test tube pregnancies."

Farmer quipped, "That's her story!"

Roger liked him so much he paid him for daily jokes after his dismissal.

WCCO Radio fired Chuck Lilligren. It was Lilligren who developed the Sunday morning Sid Hartman show. No one could put Hartman down like Lilligren.

The method of firing was horrendous. A letter went to sponsors insinuating, if not outright alleging, that Lilligren had committed grievous offenses. Lilligren sued and won a court settlement.

WCCO Radio squeezed Joe McFarlin into early retirement. Why? Because he didn't fit into management's obsession for "talk radio."

'CCO never used Joe correctly, never used his substantial talents. McFarlin could do "voices" with the best of them, and he had a rare talent for music. His own collection of rare Big Band and Traditional New Orleans records was always available. In fact, he had built a sizeable late night following all across the nation. One of the more recent management types ignored that and asked him to switch to a talk show.

WCCO Radio fired Tim Russell. Well, they forced his resignation by burying him in a graveyard shift. Tim Russell is one of the most talented radio personalities I've ever worked with. He's not only talented, he's diligent—always working to improve his skills. That's refreshing. I've seen too many talented guys get the big head and turn into prima donnas. Not Tim Russell. Squeezing him out was a decision I'll never understand.

WCCO Radio squeezed out Howard Viken, too. Never mind that he was one of the station's most popular personalities. Never mind he had produced enormous revenues for the 'CCO coffers. They just saw to it that Viken's personalized commercials dried up. Thus his income shrunk dramatically.

I've already described the Fishing Opener broadcasts. Over the years, I had done them in both Minnesota and Wisconsin since they're always separated by at least one week. My feeling was simple: How can you make a big deal out of the Minnesota fishing opener and ignore Wisconsin.

In 1993, management cancelled my plans to cover the Wisconsin opener because no sponsor could be found for the broadcasts.

That's like cancelling newscasts because they aren't sponsored.

The aforementioned AAA Weather network was unceremoniously cancelled. It was simply disbanded.

Whatever happened to the old adage, "If it ain't broke—don't fix it." Many new faces in management today (not just 'CCO management) think they have to make changes. When WCCO's ratings slumped out of the leadership for the first time in history, Roger Erickson told the Program Director, "For the first time in my life, I'm ashamed to be working here." The PD's reply, "Sorry Rog, that's the way it is—this is the way radio has to go—this is the future." I'm informed that management even had Roger Erickson on the carpet occasionally, telling him how to change his show.

*Tell Roger Erickson how to run his show!* Come on—Roger wrote the book on radio performance!

Most of these wrongs occurred in recent years. Management no longer was coming from within. The bosses didn't know the territory. They made changes for the sake of making changes. Everything became bottom line. Don't worry about putting anything back into the community. Shorten up the newscasts. Go to talk radio and stir things up à la Rush Limbaugh. I call it "in your face" radio. That's not why so many listeners for so many years called WCCO "my station"!

The CBS Network purchase of the WCCO properties had no immediate effect on ratings that were not only sagging, but in a free-fall. It's difficult to run things in the midwest from a desk back in New York. But, at least, the network sent in a trouble-shooter—and some heads rolled—rather abruptly.

The CBS Network executive in charge of all radio operations assumed temporary management of WCCO, and moved into Minneapolis. Her search for a new General Manager was lengthy. She spent much more time in the 'CCO offices than previously planned. She would wander by various departments regularly, chatting with everyone, getting to know the staff. She didn't stay at her desk, behind closed doors.

It followed that she "got to know the territory."

After selecting Jim Gustafson as the new G.M, she introduced him to a full staff assemblage. He said a few words. It was routine—until suddenly, she returned to the podium and delivered an emotional farewell. There were real tears in her eyes as she spoke of the admiration she had developed for the 'CCO staff, and gave thanks for the warmth she felt during her weeks with them.

Dick caught hundreds of Muskies
—we used to eat these beauties.

A Baracuda got half of
Barbara's Blackfin Tuna.

A Sockeye Salmon—the biggest
in Alaska that year.

Oops! That little pest again—the
smallest in Canada that year.

Sometimes both score big
(10 lb. Pompano)

**Barbara's** 47 lb. Wahoo (Queen Mackeral)

A wall mount. **Chapman's**
"S.S. Waterlog" in background

**Barbara's** 48 in. Muskie,
one of six released that day

# EPILOGUE

The next generations of WCCO Radio performers have some large shoes to fill. Some already are aboard. Dave Lee already has proven he can carry on where Roger Erickson leaves off in those wee hours of the morning. Roger Strom is a capable Maynard Speece (and Chuck Lilligren) replacement. Several women's voices brighten the WCCO Radio sound: Telly Mamayek of News, Karen Filloon of Weather, Sue Zelickson of Food and, of course, talented Ruth Koscielak. I don't know why we went so long relying only on Joyce Lamont.

Ruth Koscielak owns one of the best female voices in the business. Her voice has a smile in it—a happy sound. Were I her agent, I would press her constantly in the free-lance commercial market. The voice lends itself to selling products. This, however, becomes a detriment if she must relate grim news information. That happy sound doesn't change if she has to report a murder or a tragedy.

Karen Filloon is a genuine meteorologist, graduating from Florida State University. It must have been quite an adjustment to forecast blizzards and ice storms. She takes her craft seriously, but still manages to adjust to the repartee required when working with the likes of Cannon, Strom, Lee or others.

The news staff is as strong as ever. Eric Eskola, Steve Murphy, Bruce Hagevik, Rich Holter, Telly Mamayek, (I know I've missed some)—

all of these people have the highest professional standards. More importantly, they have the fortitude to hang in there and produce, even when things go wrong.

I know I miss the constant grouchiness of Rich Holter. We used to call him the "instant opponent"—just add water and he's against it. But he was a solid, no-nonsense newsman. When things break fast, you want him working.

I miss Bruce Hagevik's annoying habit of finishing a 5 minute news script—harshly bundling it together—then flinging it in front of me with the brusque comment, "Here—Read this!" Bruce is one of the better street reporters anywhere. Fires, disasters, murders, demonstrations—he gets there fast, gets the story, interviews the right people. His only fault is lack of brevity. He won't like that, but I always nagged him about it as I did for his propensity of choosing pretty females for interviews whenever the occasion arose.

It was Hagevik who came up with the immortal quote of the century. A bunch of us were debating the current state of affairs around WCCO Radio—arguing, griping, whatever—when suddenly (in all seriousness) Bruce said, "What we need around here is someone in charge of finding out what's going on!"

I won't forget morning News Editor Bob Wetherall and his frequent encounters with Bob DeHaven, the morning news announcer at the time. The pair loved each other, but showed it by bickering all the time—constantly trying one-upsmanship on each other. Wetherall was a wisp of a man—maybe a 130 pounder. DeHaven was huge—well over 250. Whenever Wetherall pulled a fast one on DeHaven, big Bob would pick up our huge Funk and Wagnall's Dictionary (8 inch thick, hardbound) and throw it at Wetherall. It would almost take Wetherall out of his chair. It became routine. That dictionary came to look as though it had been perused by millions of scholars over the decades—when it fact it had been thrown around too much. Nobody ever looked anything up in it.

What can be said about Eric Eskola, the fearsome Finlander. He has so much talent, it's dripping out of his ears. He's probably the best Capitol correspondent since I held the job. He's a hell of an all-around reporter too. He knows he's good (that's not to say egotistic), but he doesn't quite realize he can get even better. He doesn't realize he hasn't tapped all his talent yet. His only fault: a strange difficulty in the correct pronounciation of the letter "W." He should have picked a station with no "W's" in the call letters.

The current morning News Editor, Steve Murphy, features a carefully hidden, but always honed, sense of humor. It first arose when I was busy as hell, ranting around for a pen or pencil. I stopped at his workplace and yelled, "Your pencil or your life!"

Murphy paused.

"Well," I said.

Murphy finally replied, "I'm thinking! I'm thinking!"

It was an obvious take-off on one of the most famous gags Jack Benny ever used. That was when a stickup man threatened tightwad Jack with, "Your money or your life!"

Murphy's the Rock of Gibraltar in the newsroom. He has a Peabody Award to show for it.

During my career, I've been bugged by television's insistence on hiring anchors for their looks—men or women—makes no difference. I can't tell you how many times I've assessed the coiffures on anchors and wondered what was under those hairdos. All too often—not much. Then along came CBS's Leslie Stahl! My God! A beautiful woman with a journalistic competence par excellence! It prompted me to try waxing humorous, by paraphrasing President Roosevelt's Depression Era inaugural speech. I told my male colleagues, "What we have to fear today is not fear itself—but femininity." Many more competent, beautiful women have come along since then. My attempt at humor now rings hollow.

WCCO Radio's Telly Mamayek is an example. Never mind that she's pretty. She's as good a reporter as any man on the street, often better.

These are the kinds of people WCCO Radio must find to continue the legend. It's the most difficult task management ever faces. Hey, Management! Just don't forget to get to know the territory.

Some so-called experts (phrase borrowed from Sid Hartman) wrote A.M. Radio off many years ago. They said Television and F.M. were too much to compete with. I say hogwash!

WCCO Radio can—*and will*— prove that A.M. Radio will go on forever.

# The Society of Professional Journalists

Presents the

## Sigma Delta Chi
## Distinguished Service Award

and

Bronze  Medallion

to

## Richard Chapman

In recognition of distinguished service to the American people and the profession of journalism through outstanding accomplishment during the year of 1954 in the field of

### Radio Reporting

Victor E. Bluedorn
EXECUTIVE OFFICER

Alden C. Waik
NATIONAL PRESIDENT

Acknowledgments

Thank you to the many friends and colleagues who provided information and experiences that made this book so much fun to write. Special thanks to Jack Hansen for figuring out what had to be done, when and how, to get published; to Marjorie Owen for proofreading; to Barbara Chapman for editing and formatting; and to Donna and Gerry Smith, MaryJo Mazzitelli and Kathy Krom for professional technical assistance at SOS Printing in Mound.

Printed at
S•O•S PRINTING, INC
2361 WILSHIRE BLVD.
MOUND, MN 55364

# INDEX